Morning

&

Evening

Devotions During Lent

By Rev. Guillaume J. S. Williams, Sr.

Contents

Preface

Morning & Evening is a devotional book covering the time of Lent in the Church year. The recommended readings come from the Daily Lectionary which can be found in the Lutheran Service Book. It assumed you would read one reading in the morning and one in the evening. It is set up to read the Old Testament lesson in the morning and the New Testament lesson in the evening. If you are using my other book Pray Unceasingly, you may want to use the longer reading for the chapter reading of one office and the devotion for the chapter reading of another office, depending on how you are using that breviary's options.

Now it should be noted that this is not a commentary and is not meant to be one. A devotional is meant to focus on a verse or several verses and the reading that follows is to help us to guide our hearts and minds toward heavenly things. Its purpose is to help us to grow spiritually and to think deeply about that scripture passage. If you disagree with the direction of the devotion that is still a good thing because it got you thinking about it. The Holy Spirit may have your thoughts move in a completely different direction from the devotion because that is what you need to understand at the time.

This devotional is meant to be read in a conversational tone. You will find the language and syntax to be very colloquial. We are having a conversation. If sentence fragments bother you, consider this to be a spiritual exercise of tolerance.

If you want to use this devotional in a larger context of worship may I share with you what I do with my family? You may have some of this in your worship bulletin from the previous Sunday. The collects can also be found in The Lutheran Hymnal and Lutheran Worship or perhaps whatever hymnal you have at home. If have trouble finding them ask your pastor. Another resource for Collects of the Day of the Church Season may be found here:
https://weedon.blogspot.com/2006/10/collects-for-free.html
Invocation
10 Commandments
The Apostles' Creed
The Hymn of the Day from the Previous Sunday
The Reading
The Devotion
The Collect of the Day from Sunday
The Lord's Prayer
Luther's Morning or Evening Prayer

It is my prayer this devotional will be helpful for your spiritual life and will draw to closer to our Lord Jesus Christ and Our Father in heaven through the Word and Spirit.

Ash Wednesday

Read Gen 1:1–19

Gen 1:1-2 In the beginning, God created the heavens and the earth. (2) The earth was without form and void, and darkness was over the face of the deep. And the Spirit of God was hovering over the face of the waters.

There's a lot of tension at times between Christians and Scientist. Well that's not true entirely. There is tension between Scientist who believe science has all the answers and possesses the only way to any and all sorts of knowledge and Christians who don't understand that science, true science, only explains what it sees and can observe now and use those facts to postulate backwards in time as to how we got how we are.

Now creation, that is, faith in what God's word has to say about it I believe happened just as God describes it in chapter one of Genesis. God created a world, a universe with all its parts and he created it complete. Since that is the case, I don't believe it is the case that he is being deceitful. It isn't his intent to deceive. But he created it will all the laws of the universe so we can observe nature and project it forwards and know what we can expect. It just so happens, if you can project forwards, you can project backwards as well. Except when you project backwards with the completeness we have today, you are going to get an old universe.

That aside, it does take faith to believe God created the heavens and the earth, as it is written, Heb 11:3 "By faith we understand that the universe was created by the word of God, so that what is seen was not made out of things that are visible." As an article of faith, we can never prove scientifically God did it. Logically we can prove God made the universe though.

Creation is a good thing. It is created for us! God didn't need it. Yet the three persons of the Trinity, the Father, the Son and the Holy Spirit were intimately involved with making this creation for us. Imagine the mind of God and power of God who is able to this universe and everything in it. In today's reading we get light, the heavens, dry ground, vegetation and lights in the heavens. How wonderful and marvelous it all is. And yet today we are called to repent. Paul writes, Rom 1:21 "For although they knew God, they did not honor him as God or give thanks to him, but they became futile in their thinking, and their foolish hearts were darkened." At times we forget God made all this for us. We forget Word, Jesus, created and arraigned all this. We oppose at times the Holy Spirit and do not honor God or give thanks to him for this creation. We turn to created things instead of God for every good. This day, let us return to God with penitent hearts, confessing our idolatry of worldly goods and ask for forgiveness for the sake of Jesus Christ our Lord and Savior.

Heavenly Father, we give you thanks and praise for all of creation. Help us always to recognize and believe all you have made for us. Give us a spirit of devotion that looks only to you for all good things and recognizes you as the giver of every good gift. In Jesus' name we pray. Amen.

Ash Wednesday
Read Mark 1:1–13
Mar 1:4-5 John appeared, baptizing in the wilderness and proclaiming a baptism of repentance for the forgiveness of sins. (5) And all the country of Judea and all Jerusalem were going out to him and were being baptized by him in the river Jordan, confessing their sins.

We begin our Lenten season with the proclamation of the Gospel through John. John was doing something amazing. He was proclaiming a baptism of repentance for the forgiveness of sins. While we do not have whole sermons of John the sum and content of them was repent for the kingdom of God is at hand. Repent, have a change of heart, turn away from sin and be baptized for the forgiveness of sins. They came to John confessing their sins as a sign of their repentance. Then he bestowed the kingdom of God upon them by baptizing with them. When they were baptized they were initiated into the kingdom.

Today, we begin this season doing something we ought to be doing all year. We confess our sins and trust in Christ' promise that whoever believes and is baptized will be saved. But sometimes we forget so we have these Church seasons to remind us. So maybe today, take out pen and paper. Take an inventory of your last year. What have you done apart from the will of God? Did you lack in praying or going to Church? Were you only going through the motions when you were there and not paying attention to the gifts Christ was giving you? How have you hurt or harmed your neighbor, your spouse, your kids, your employers or employees? Are there any wicked habits you have developed?

Now that you've got them written down, do what the people who heard John did, go to your pastor and confess your sins. He will bestow upon you a great gift that will help you to remove the power of these sins from your life. What might this gift be? Well if you are already baptized he will in the stead and by the command of Christ forgive you your sins. Jesus bestowed this gift to the Church when he said to his disciples, John 20:22… "Receive the Holy Spirit. (23) If you forgive the sins of any, they are forgiven them; if you withhold forgiveness from any, it is withheld."

Don't be afraid. He isn't there to judge you. You are judging yourself there's no need for him to judge you. He is there to speak the comforting words of Christ, "Your sins are forgiven you."

Lord Jesus Christ, John prepared the way for you proclaiming a baptism of repentance for the forgiveness of sins. Grant us your Holy Spirit that we may rightly judge our sins, confess them and receive the gift of forgiveness in your name. Amen.

2nd day of Lent Thursday
Read 1:20—2:3
Gen 1:31-2:3 And God saw everything that he had made, and behold, it was very good. And there was evening and there was morning, the sixth day. (2:1) Thus the heavens and the earth were finished, and all the host of them. (2) And on the seventh day God finished his work that he had done, and he rested on the seventh day from all his work that he had done. (3) So God blessed the seventh day and made it holy, because on it God rested from all his work that he had done in creation.

When God had finished creating everything he declared it very good. Every day when he ended his work, it was good, but the whole thing together is very good. Kind of makes you wonder what happened sometimes doesn't it. Believe it or not, it is still very good for St. Paul writes, 1Ti 4:4-5 "For everything created by God is good, and nothing is to be rejected if it is received with thanksgiving, (5) for it is made holy by the word of God and prayer." God is not the author of evil. In fact evil has no existence of its own. It is an accident. It is like a dent on the car. My fender can exist without a dent, but the dent, unfortunately, cannot exist without my fender…and too often it does exist.

Now God rested from his work. It was the seventh day. Now does God need a rest? No. this rest is for our sakes. It is written, Heb 3:11 "As I swore in my wrath, 'They shall not enter my rest.'" It has been noted there is not an end to the Sabbath day in Genesis two. God's rest is eternal. He intends for humanity to enter that rest. Hebrews tells us, Heb 4:1 "Therefore, while the promise of entering his rest still stands, let us fear lest any of you should seem to have failed to reach it." And again, Heb 4:7 "… he appoints a certain day, "Today," saying through David so long afterward, in the words already quoted, "Today, if you hear his voice, do not harden your hearts."

We enter that rest in repentance of our lack of faith and trust in God. We confess that we have either set ourselves up as God sometimes or look to created things to play that part and have sinned against God. Even more so we look to Jesus who was tempted for our sake yet overcame the tempter. Jesus' victory is our victory. So we look to Jesus as the one who atones for our sins and as the one who is victorious over temptation as wel

God has a rest planned for you. Even now, with faith in Christ, we already begin to rest from our works and rest in the works of Christ Jesus our Lord.

Heavenly Father, grant unto us such repentance and faith in your Son Jesus Christ that we may rest from our works and enter into your rest today and for eternity. In Jesus' name. Amen.

2nd day of Lent
Read Mark 1:14–28
Mar 1:14-15 Now after John was arrested, Jesus came into Galilee, proclaiming the gospel of God, (15) and saying, "The time is fulfilled, and the kingdom of God is at hand; repent and believe in the gospel."

Jesus begins his ministry proclaiming the same message as John the Baptist, ""The time is fulfilled, and the kingdom of God is at hand; repent and believe in the gospel." Though Jesus' message is slightly different here. John was preparing for the kingdom of God to come and Jesus brings the kingdom of God with him. But Jesus' message is the same in that he calls us to all to repent and believe the good news of the kingdom i.e. the kingdom of God is here.

We see clearly what that means when Jesus first proclaims the Word of God with power and then cast out a demon. For that is the power and the coming of the kingdom of God. It is to wreck havoc on the kingdom of Satan and the World which serves him. For this world's god is Satan. All people everywhere serve him if they are not serving Jesus. Jesus came to cast out Satan and his dominion over mankind.

The good news is that in Christ Jesus we no longer have to serve Satan. We can be free of his dominion. Sure it is true while we are in this world we still have his influence over our sinful flesh and the world around us. But we are no longer his puppets. With faith in Christ Jesus, through the waters of Holy Baptism, we have a new inhabitant of our bodies, the Holy Spirit. We have become the temples of God. Since we have been freed from the power of Satan we are no longer to give ourselves over to our sinful desires and give Satan room again in our lives. It is a struggle to be sure. If it wasn't it wouldn't be called temptation.

So our fortress in those times of temptation is prayer to the Father in Jesus' name. We need to trust God is with us. We need to believe Jesus' promise our sins are forgiven us and separated from us as far as East is from the West. We need to call on fellow believers to assist us in our fighting of temptations for they are one body with us. And should we fall into temptation, confess our sin and ask for forgiveness trusting it is there for us on account of Jesus. Don't fall for the devil's lie that you've gone too far now and God can't and won't forgive you. That is the devil's little trap.

Lord Jesus Christ may your kingdom come in our lives that we give no quarter to Satan in our hearts but that our hearts would be filled with your Holy Spirit. Amen.

3rd day of Lent Friday
Read Gen 2:4–25
Gen 2:16-24 And the LORD God commanded the man, saying, "You may surely eat of every tree of the garden, (17) but of the tree of the knowledge of good and evil you shall not eat, for in the day that you eat of it you shall surely die." (18) Then the LORD God said, "It is not good that the man should be alone; I will make him a helper fit for him."

We have two major things happening in this section of Genesis and the creation account. First is the set up of man's ultimate fall. We really don't know why God decided to place in the garden two trees of which the man could choose to eat and forbidding him to eat one of them. So it is of no use speculating why. What we do know is all God wanted Adam to do was not eat the fruit of the tree of good and evil. We note God didn't say he couldn't chop it down. He didn't say he could build a tree house in it. Nor did God say he couldn't have a food fight with the fruit. He simply could not eat the fruit.

There is then the grave threat that if he did eat it, on that day he would die. Now we read this and knowing the rest of the account know Adam does eat it and he lives another 900 years. What gives? Just this, God doesn't view death like us. The death he is referring to is the removal of his life, his spirit; his soul dies on that day.

The second major part is the creation of woman. Like in this whole account of the creation of man in chapter 2 it is a very personal and hands on creation of mankind. Just as God creates man from the dust of the earth and breathes his life into man, now he takes a rib out of man and forms from it woman, a suitable helper. God had brought all the animals to the man first to see what he would name them. There was no suitable helper among them, not even the dog. Even a six-pack of beer isn't suitable for the man.

So God takes a part of man from him and actually makes something or rather someone suitable for the man. Adam upon receiving this wonderful gift from God names her-demonstrating his superior position (but not in a sinful way but in an order of creation way) and calls her woman because she was taken from man. While I do not know every language of mankind it is interesting to note of all the languages I do know, every word for woman contains the name for man.

Man really appreciates and glories in this gift that he breaks forth into poetry. And we receive this principle here for marriage we in our culture need to take to heart. A marriage is between a man and a woman. Secondly, when you are married you become one flesh even as God is Father, Son and Holy Spirit yet one God. What this means is you are to stick to your spouse and defend your spouse even above your own originating family. Parents, family and friends are not to come between a married couple and married couples shouldn't let them interfere in the marriage.

Lord God, heavenly Father, we thank you for the gift of creation and for the gift of marriage. Help all married couples honor their marriage bed and keep all single people chaste until such time as you joined them to another. In Jesus' Name we pray, amen.

3rd day of Lent Friday

Read Mark 1:29–45

Mar 1:38-44 And he said to them, "Let us go on to the next towns, that I may preach there also, for that is why I came out." (39) And he went throughout all Galilee, preaching in their synagogues and casting out demons. (40) And a leper came to him, imploring him, and kneeling said to him, "If you will, you can make me clean." (41) Moved with pity, he stretched out his hand and touched him and said to him, "I will; be clean."

In today's lesson we see a several things we ought to which we ought to pay attention. One is verse 38 which is key. We want to pay attention to the casting out of demons and the healings. Those are important because they testify that Jesus' message is authoritative. They demonstrate the power of the Word. But what is most important is that Jesus says He came to preach. It is through the preaching of repentance and forgiveness of sins the kingdom of God was invading and taking over enemy space. The miracles are merely testimonies of that happening. Jesus preached the law and made people feel quite guilty and upset over their sins. His preaching terrified sinners. But he also preached forgiveness for those very same sins and by doing so he took away the power of the evil one.

Third, we note that Jesus full of pity and mercy. He really feels this for you even as he did the leper. He may not always display that mercy in the same way as he has done the leper in this life. His promise is for the next world though sometimes he does intervene in this time and space when it will give glory to the gospel and confirm people in the faith. Jesus' mission today is still to preach repentance and forgiveness.

Finally, Jesus is not the big rabble rouser some people like to make him out to be. He respected the authorities, religious and political. Note what he does when he heals the leper. He sends him to the priest to fulfill the Law of Moses. Jesus is not against institutions. In fact he sets them up. He has set up the Church. He has given us pastors (Eph. 4:11) and the Church. He doesn't want us side-stepping it. It is his body and his bride. It is there he preaches to us the same message he preached before his crucifixion, death and resurrection.

The kingdom comes into the world now as his pastors preach the good news of forgiveness of sins for the sake of Jesus Christ. They preach why we need forgiveness, we break God's law and they preach to us the solution which delivers us from the dominion of darkness. Find someplace where this is happening.

Lord Jesus Christ, you established your kingdom on earth with your preaching of the Kingdom and demonstrated it with power. Grant us faith to continue to preach the kingdom and believe your promises even without miraculous signs. Amen.

Lent Day 4 Saturday

Read Gen 3:1–24

Gen 3:1 Now the serpent was more crafty than any other beast of the field that the LORD God had made. He said to the woman, "Did God actually say, 'You shall not eat of any tree in the garden'?" Gen 3:13 Then the LORD God said to the woman, "What is this that you have done?" The woman said, "The serpent deceived me, and I ate." (14) The LORD God said to the serpent, "Because you have done this, cursed are you above all livestock and above all beasts of the field; on your belly you shall go, and dust you shall eat all the days of your life. (15) I will put enmity between you and the woman, and between your offspring and her offspring; he shall bruise your head, and you shall bruise his heel."

First we ought to note how the devil works. He tries to get us to doubt God's word and he does it by quoting God's word. We of course don't want to sound like dolts and so we try to reason with him, or our hearts or the person we're talking with. You will lose if you engage beyond what God said. It is probably better to do what Jesus did and simply say, "Get behind me Satan!" And then move on.

Now look at the seriousness of what sin does. It doesn't matter what sin, of how much you think it doesn't really hurt you or hurt your neighbor. You are not the one to judge whether not something forbidden or commanded by God is serious or not. What did Adam and Eve do—on the surface? They ate a piece of fruit! THAT'S IT!? All this misery and death and the world is because they ate a piece of fruit?

Well no. But that is what the devil, the world and your sinful heart would want you to believe. No what brought this misery upon creation was that they DISOBEYED God and didn't TRUST Him. You see all sin is not trusting God at his word and disobeying him. THAT is a big thing because you're sinning against a BIG guy. You see, I could punch you and not much would come of it. I punch the POTUS and I land in the jail. What's the difference? The president is more important than you. God is the most important of all. It doesn't matter how small the offense you think it is. It is against God. That's all that matters. The other thing we ought to note is the blame game. Adam blamed the woman and God. The woman blamed the snake and the snake didn't have leg to stand on. Take responsibility for your own sins.

There is good news here. God promises to send a savior born of the Woman's seed. That Woman is Mary and that Savior is Jesus. By his death at the hand of Satan, he defeats Satan by quashing his head. Trust this and God will cover you not with animal skins but the righteousness of Jesus.

Lord God, heavenly Father give us such faith in Jesus that we listen, trust and obey and ignore Satan, death and our hearts. In Jesus' name we pray, Amen.

Lent Day 4 Saturday
Read Mark 2:1–17
Mar 2:5-7 And when Jesus saw their faith, he said to the paralytic, "Son, your sins are forgiven." (6) Now some of the scribes were sitting there, questioning in their hearts, (7) "Why does this man speak like that? He is blaspheming! Who can forgive sins but God alone?"

Who hasn't heard such stuff from visitors from other faiths or should it come up in a conversation with them. We hear the pastor absolve us of our sins. Our flesh says, "This can't be!" Our neighbors, religious or otherwise think the same thing the scribes were thinking, "He is blaspheming!" It is because they neither know God nor scripture. They all think you have to earn God's forgiveness. Grace isn't grace at all for them. It isn't a gift for them.

But back to the story, Jesus forgives the man and can do it without blaspheming because he is very God of very God. Jesus is the fullness of God in bodily form. He has every right and power to forgive, because all sins are committed are committed against him. In the flesh though, Jesus does something else particularly for the bean counting type. Jesus goes and earns forgiveness for mankind. Jesus speaks as the one who will shed his blood for the atoning of this man's and all mankind's sin. We may put off Jesus' pronouncement because it is easy to say when we don't see anything happen. But that they may know that Jesus does have authority to forgive sins he actually does the easier thing, he heals the man. The healing is the fruit of the forgiveness. At the resurrection we shall see the fruit of the forgiveness won by Christ in our risen bodies. We think the healing is the big thing but the forgiveness Christ pronounces requires his very life.

Now in order that we might receive this forgiveness Jesus establishes the holy ministry. John 20:22-23 And when he had said this, he breathed on them and said to them, "Receive the Holy Spirit. (23) If you forgive the sins of any, they are forgiven them; if you withhold forgiveness from any, it is withheld." As Jesus ascends to the right hand of the Father, he sends pastors into the world with his authority as ambassadors to the world. As his ambassadors his message through them is forgiveness. While the world and religious may mock them thinking they are blaspheming, they are delivering the greatest message, the greatest gift, the cure to all ills, and the cure even to death. It is the free gift of the forgiveness of sins on account of the life, death and resurrection of Jesus Christ.

Dearest Jesus, send us your ambassadors who proclaim to us the forgiveness of sins freely for your sake. Give us your Holy Spirit that we might believe them and enter into glory with you as you have promised. Amen.

1st Sunday in Lent

Gen 4:1–26

Gen 4:1 Now Adam knew Eve his wife, and she conceived and bore Cain, saying, "I have gotten a man with the help of the LORD."

Gen 4:15 Then the LORD said to him, "Not so! If anyone kills Cain, vengeance shall be taken on him sevenfold." And the LORD put a mark on Cain, lest any who found him should attack him.

In the Hebrew it is apparent that Eve believed the threat God made to the serpent. The literal reading of the text reads, "I have given birth to a man, the Lord." She believed Cain was the promised seed who would crush the head of the serpent. Unfortunately this would not be the case, though she certainly still thought this at the birth of Able naming him worthless. There was no need for another male child. Eve understood a seed from her womb would be the Messiah who is also her Creator.

Now a woman's seed would be the Messiah. It would be without the help of a male. Isaiah prophesied he would be born of a virgin. Indeed the Messiah has been born of a Virgin, the Woman's seed. Her name is Mary. His name is Jesus. Jesus means 'the Lord saves.' That is exactly what Jesus did. Jesus on the cross was struck by the serpent at the hand of the Romans and the Jews. But in that act, Jesus crushed the head of the serpent. He took the devil's power away to accuse us before God and to compel us to sin. By his resurrection Jesus defeated death and the one who has the power over death, the devil. Now all who put their faith in the Messiah, Jesus of Nazareth, the son of Mary, the Son of God, possess eternal life.

But what about Cain? Cain was worried he would be killed by others for killing his brother. The Lord assures him this will not happen. He places a mark on Cain so he would not be attacked. Just what was that mark? Many believe it was a Tau, a Hebrew letter which resembles a cross. When we baptize people, we place the mark of the cross upon the heart and head of the baptized to mark them as one who has been redeemed by the crucified one. Cain received a mark of life which is a sign of death. Was he repentant? I think so, which is why God showed this mercy to him. What have you done that perhaps you fear reprisals from your fellow man? What have you done that perhaps you fear the judgment of God?

God does not want to punish you. He does not want you to die eternally. He has provided a Seed of a Woman to redeem you, to ransom you, to atone for your sins, your guilt and your shame. Place your trust in God's promise that he has done this for you and you too shall receive the mark of the one crucified, Jesus Christ. Then you will no longer fear death or the devil. He cannot permanently harm you. You will have eternal life and will have gained immortality.

Heavenly Father, we thank you for providing for us one who has had victory over sin, death and the devil. Grant us faith always to trust in this one, Jesus Christ, that we may not live in fear but in faith your goodness, mercy and kindness. In Jesus' name we pray. Amen.

1st Sunday in Lent
Read Mark 2:18–28
Mar 2:27-28 And he said to them, "The Sabbath was made for man, not man for the Sabbath. (28) So the Son of Man is lord even of the Sabbath."

There are two issues which are really one issue in this lesson. The subject of fasting and the subject of the Sabbath are taken up. Now the Pharisees fasted twice a week, Tuesday and Thursday. John's disciples fasted. Jesus' disciples did not fast. The disciples were picking grain and eating it on the Sabbath. The Pharisees determined this was work.

In both cases, Jesus is clarifying the Law of Moses. Nowhere in the Law or the Prophets were God's people ever commanded to fast twice a week. Indeed, there was only one commanded fast. And the fast the Pharisees and others may have practiced was not according to God's will. God did not count what the disciples were doing as work. Now Jesus clarifies the Law with these words, The Sabbath was made for man, not man for the Sabbath."

The Law of God is not for His benefit. God does not need the Law. Man on the other does need the Law. It is for man's benefit that God gave the Law. Now we know the sum of the Law is "Love your neighbor as yourself." Love is the fulfillment of the Law. So as we go about our Christian lives we may be faced with a quandary, either break God's law or prevent injury to another human being. What should we do? We help our fellow man. Helping our fellow man is always good.

Now I am not saying that we condone sin. Most of the time any sin causes harm to us and to others. God does not want us to harm others. The moral law still stands. But when someone's health and well being is in danger, God wants us to make that a priority. So Jesus heals the man on the Sabbath who has an injured hand. Likewise, we pull over to help people on the way to Church. We forgo having lunch or dinner one day to provide food for another. We take our extra clothes and clothe someone who has none or isn't proper for the season.

When we have failed in loving our neighbor and the Lord, we have an advocate with the Father, the Son of Man, our Lord Jesus Christ. We confess our sin to him and receive from him his mercy, kindness and love. He knows we are often confused and conflicted and we fall short of doing his will. So he shows us the love that we need in fulfilling the Law for us and dying, paying the price of our sin and removes the curse of the law for us. Now we can live in the freedom of the Lord and fulfill the will of God in faith.

Heavenly Father, help us always to show love to our neighbor. Grant us your Holy Spirit that we may understand your will in our lives and live our live according to the grace and mercy found in Christ Jesus. In Jesus' name we pray. Amen.

Lent Day 5 Monday
Read Gen 6:1—7:5

Gen 6:5-9 The LORD saw that the wickedness of man was great in the earth, and that every intention of the thoughts of his heart was only evil continually. (6) And the LORD was sorry that he had made man on the earth, and it grieved him to his heart. (7) So the LORD said, "I will blot out man whom I have created from the face of the land, man and animals and creeping things and birds of the heavens, for I am sorry that I have made them." (8) But Noah found favor in the eyes of the LORD. (9) These are the generations of Noah. Noah was a righteous man, blameless in his generation. Noah walked with God.

It's unfortunate I guess that nothing changed after the flood. Jesus said, Mat 15:19 "For out of the heart come evil thoughts, murder, adultery, sexual immorality, theft, false witness, slander." The natural man since the fall intends only evil continually. Jesus tells us what we want to do. Because this was the case before the flood, God decided to wipe out most of mankind. I guess it finally got too much for God and his patience had finally worn out with them. It grieved God's heart that he had made us. Not only mankind but even all the birds and land animals He is going to wipe out.

But God is also merciful towards His creation. One man finds favor with the Lord and that man is Noah. God describes him as "a righteous man, blameless in his generation." What made Noah righteous and blameless? Faith. Among all the people on earth only Noah that we know of, had faith in God. We don't know about his wife, kids or daughters in law. But Noah had faith.

The Bible says, Heb 11:6-7 "And without faith it is impossible to please him, for whoever would draw near to God must believe that he exists and that he rewards those who seek him. (7) By faith Noah, being warned by God concerning events as yet unseen, in reverent fear constructed an ark for the saving of his household. By this he condemned the world and became an heir of the righteousness that comes by faith." The world was condemned because they did not believe his preaching.

The Lord has told us the end is coming again, this time with fire. The ark that God has sent to save us is His Church. Jesus is the new Noah. He has preached and he continues to preach salvation to all who are changed in their minds and believe in His name or His works will be saved. These people are those who are blameless and righteous in God's sight.

Lord God, heavenly Father, grant us ears to hear the Noahs you send to us that we may repent, believe the gospel and escape the coming fire. In Jesus' name we pray, amen.

Lent Day 5 Monday
Mark 3:1–19
Mar 3:3-4 And he said to the man with the withered hand, "Come here." (4) And he said to them, "Is it lawful on the Sabbath to do good or to do harm, to save life or to kill?" But they were silent.

What does this tell us? On the one hand you weren't supposed to work on the Sabbath. On the other hand you are to love our neighbor as yourself. Well, it may appear we would have to break one law in order to keep the other. The law is not given for God. He doesn't need us. Any laws concerning Him are for our benefit, not his. But we have his image in front of us.

John writes, 1Jn 4:20 "If anyone says, "I love God," and hates his brother, he is a liar; for he who does not love his brother whom he has seen cannot love God whom he has not seen." John and Paul both tell us love your neighbor is fulfilling the Law. So if you have a choice between obeying a law towards God or loving your neighbor who is the image of God, love your neighbor. God can handle it. Jesus loved his neighbor.

If we are helping our neighbor, indeed we are not breaking the commandment but actually keeping it. Our help brings our neighbor relief. It brings our neighbor to a point of rest. It gives him an opportunity to praise and give thanks to God. We glorify Christ by doing good to our neighbor and showing him God's love. Now of course we are not bound by the Mosaic laws, rules, statutes, regulations and judgments. We live under a new covenant: One won and written by and in the blood of Jesus. As people who live in the new covenant, we should not be sticklers for rules that were written to help us if they force us to not show love to the neighbor. We have, in Jesus, our Sabbath rest, come to rest from our works and live and do the works of God. Those are to trust Jesus and to love our neighbor as ourselves.

Heavenly Father, when it is difficult to know what to do, give us your Holy Spirit so that we may discern how we may best serve our neighbor and by doing so serve and love you. Amen.

Lent Day 6th Tuesday
Read Gen 7:11—8:12

1Gen 7:13 On the very same day Noah and his sons, Shem and Ham and Japheth, and Noah's wife and the three wives of his sons with them entered the ark…23 He blotted out every living thing that was on the face of the ground, man and animals and creeping things and birds of the heavens. They were blotted out from the earth. Only Noah was left, and those who were with him in the ark….Gen 8:1 But God remembered Noah and all the beasts and all the livestock that were with him in the ark. And God made a wind blow over the earth, and the waters subsided.

Many unbelievers and a few believers at that, look at this event from Genesis with horror. What kind of God would kill every man, woman and child and every beast of the earth just because they were sinful? They may understand every man and woman, but child and beasts? What a cruel God, they think. They have heard God is love but where is the love in this?

But they and we sometimes do not understand the true nature of sin. It has corrupted all people and all creation. While we may look around and see good stuff happening around us, we cannot see into the hearts of people and we can just turn on the TV and see how it affects our world. We must look at this lesson and look at our world and repent before God comes again in judgment but not by a flood but with fire at the revelation of Jesus Christ.

But God is love and God is merciful and kind. It is not kind and loving to let sin continue to rule people's lives and to let them to continue to debase themselves, others and the world. God is merciful and kind because as we see in chapter 7 he preserves mankind, eight people in all to continue humanity. He could have decided, and rightly so, to wipe us all out and just start over with a new lump of clay. But we are here because of his mercy, kindness and love towards humanity. He preserved the animals of the earth by saving 7 pairs of clean animals according to their kind and one pair of unclean animals according to their kind.

God is loving, merciful and kind because he remembered Noah, his family and the beasts aboard the ark. He dissipated the water so they could have a new life as God renewed the face of the earth. When Christ comes, he too will remember his people who live in the ark of the Church. He shall raise them bodily and change our lowly bodies to be like his. He will renew the cosmos as he takes all wickedness from it. It will be a world where righteousness reigns. He promises this to all who repent of their sins and trust in for their salvation. It is for who are baptized and believe on him for eternal life.

Are you going to be like those outside the ark and mock God's people or are you going to trust Christ' word and join his people in the safety of the ark, the Church?

Heavenly Father, ever give us true repentant and faith in Jesus' words of promise that we may be held safely in the ark of your Church until his revelation on the Last Day. In Jesus' name we pray. Amen.

Lent Day 6th Tuesday
Read Mark 3:20–35

Mar 3:21 And when his family heard it, they went out to seize him, for they were saying, "He is out of his mind."… 3:33 And he answered them, "Who are my mother and my brothers?" (34) And looking about at those who sat around him, he said, "Here are my mother and my brothers! (35) For whoever does the will of God, he is my brother and sister and mother."

Even Jesus had a rough time with his family. In this passage they think he is out of his mind. In John chapter seven, his brothers mock him. As Christians, even if we don't have the best family according to the flesh. They may not support you in your life as a Christian. Maybe they don't support you in any way at all. You may feel lonely and alone amongst your own blood relatives. Jesus at this point may certainly have felt that way.

Jesus points us though to a new family. That family is the Church. Those who do the will of God are his family. What is God's will? That you believe in Jesus Christ whom God the Father sent and to love your neighbor as yourself. Jesus looks at those people following him and points them out to be his mother and his brothers and sisters. These were not perfect people by a long shot. When you came to faith in Jesus, you too became part of Jesus' family.

Jesus will later tell us in Mark, Mar 10:29-30 Jesus said, "Truly, I say to you, there is no one who has left house or brothers or sisters or mother or father or children or lands, for my sake and for the gospel, (30) who will not receive a hundredfold now in this time, houses and brothers and sisters and mothers and children and lands, with persecutions, and in the age to come eternal life."

So we have this comfort in Christ, when the world, our communities and even our family abandon us, when we have faith in Jesus, we are part of his family. Jesus will never abandon us. We will gain back a new family, even in this life, when we become part of his Church. We never have to feel lonely or alone again. Comfort is only a phone call away most of the time. Strength to face life in this world is among Christ Jesus' family here.

Heavenly Father, we give you thanks that through the gift of faith in your Son Jesus Christ. Ever keep us in this faith that we may experience now and in the world to come the comfort of being considered your holy family. In Jesus' name. Amen.

Lent Day 7 Wednesday
Read Gen 8:13—9:17

Gen 8:21 And when the LORD smelled the pleasing aroma, the LORD said in his heart, "I will never again curse the ground because of man, for the intention of man's heart is evil from his youth. Neither will I ever again strike down every living creature as I have done…9:1 And God blessed Noah and his sons and said to them, "Be fruitful and multiply and fill the earth…14 When I bring clouds over the earth and the bow is seen in the clouds, (15) I will remember my covenant that is between me and you and every living creature of all flesh. And the waters shall never again become a flood to destroy all flesh.

Here we see the kindness of God despite our sinfulness. Our true, fallen nature is told us here. If God did not reveal it to us, we would not believe it. He tells us, "the intention of man's heart is evil from his youth." The Lord is just repeating what he said a couple of chapters previously, "Gen 6:5 The LORD saw that the wickedness of man was great in the earth, and that every intention of the thoughts of his heart was only evil continually." It is a rather bleak picture of man. This isn't the only place the Scriptures speak like this. David writes, Psa 51:5 "Behold, I was brought forth in iniquity, and in sin did my mother conceive me." From the moment of conception we are sinful. Our every intention, our every desire is to do evil continually. The New Testament confesses the same thing. Paul tells us, Eph 2:3 "…we …were by nature children of wrath, like the rest of mankind." Jesus doesn't help our self-image either. He tells us, "Mat 15:19 For out of the heart come evil thoughts, murder, adultery, sexual immorality, theft, false witness, slander."

In God's great kindness and love for us, he preserves mankind despite our sinfulness. He gives us a promise, a promise he doesn't have to give. He promises he will never kill every creature on the earth, including mankind, like he did here in Genesis. He gives us a sign to look to whenever we may fear that, a rainbow. It is a sign of the covenant God has made with us that he will never flood the whole earth again.

The Lord has also given us another sign that he desires to be merciful to us. That sign is Jesus. As weird as it may seem, the sign of his love for us is Jesus hanging on a tree, on a cross. Jesus tells us, John 3:14-15 "And as Moses lifted up the serpent in the wilderness, so must the Son of Man be lifted up, (15) that whoever believes in him may have eternal life." Jesus lifted up is God's sign of mercy to us. Whoever looks to Jesus' cross and believes there God has made peace with us need not fear the wrath God when he destroys the earth again but with fire. 2 Pet. 3:7 Any time of day you think God has abandoned you because of your sin, look to a tree, a telephone pole, if you are desperate, any two intersecting lines and remember that God, in his great love for you, gave his son Jesus as a peace offering. He no longer counts your trespasses against you. God is please because of the aroma from the sacrifice of the cross.

Heavenly Father, give us always the faith to believe in your covenant of peace you made with us by Jesus' crucifixion that our hearts may find comfort wherever we look and see the sign of the covenant of your great love for us. In Jesus' name. Amen.

Lent day 7 Wednesday
Read Mark 4:1–20
Mar 4:20 But those that were sown on the good soil are the ones who hear the word and accept it and bear fruit, thirtyfold and sixtyfold and a hundredfold."

I always found it interesting that the explanation of the parable seems to leave out something. Perhaps we are to intuit it ourselves. We get that Satan doesn't allow some people to receive the Word. We get that in times of persecution some people will simply choose to escape persecution by denying Jesus. We get that sometimes things, the happenings of life will pull us away from faith in Christ by neglecting the gathering of the Saints.

What we don't seem to get is the good soil. We must understand that the soil represents different types of people and their circumstances. But really, it is not like the good soil doesn't have Satan attacking it. Perhaps he's actually working on it more. It's not like the good soil doesn't undergo persecution. We see a pastor in Iran facing death for the face, yet it appears he is still good soil. There millions of faithful who actually do live in the real world (where else would they live) who face life and the cares of life who do not drift away from Christ. The good soil is that which remain faithful to Christ and bears the fruit of the Spirit. Why is that?

It comes down to the grace of God and some things are simply beyond our understanding. But I believe this parable is given us to encourage us to remain faithful no matter what. Whatever is thrown at you, do not give up on Christ. If you do not give up before the miracle happens you will bear an abundant fruit of righteousness. It simply comes down to trusting Christ even when it doesn't seem like it's worth it. When faith seems to fail we remain faithful.

And remember that it is when you seem that you are on your last leg, well maybe even that last leg has been taken out from underneath you that the Lord does his best work. Mary sings, "Luk 1:52-53 he has brought down the mighty from their thrones and exalted those of humble estate; (53) he has filled the hungry with good things, and the rich he has sent away empty." James writes, "Jas 4:10 Humble yourselves before the Lord, and he will exalt you." Peter confirms, 1Pe 5:6 Humble yourselves, therefore, under the mighty hand of God so that at the proper time he may exalt you…" Finally Jesus tells Paul, 2Co 12:9 "My grace is sufficient for you, for my power is made perfect in weakness."

Good soil is weeded, plowed under, pummeled, drilled, sometimes even set fire. It isn't easy becoming good soil. It is a work of God. But the soil along the way, the thorny soil and the rocky soil it does not humble itself under the hand of God and seeks an easier, softer way.

Lord Jesus Christ, continually give us your Holy Spirit that we may be good soil, remain faithful to the end and bear a harvest of righteousness. Amen.

Lent Day 8 Thursday
Read 11:27—12:20
Gen 12:1-3 Now the LORD said to Abram, "Go from your country and your kindred and your father's house to the land that I will show you. (2) And I will make of you a great nation, and I will bless you and make your name great, so that you will be a blessing. (3) I will bless those who bless you, and him who dishonors you I will curse, and in you all the families of the earth shall be blessed."

As the numbers of people increase upon the land God narrows down through whom the blessing spoken about the Woman in Gen. 3:15 would come about. The seed of the Woman would come through the seed of Abram (Abraham).

God sends Abram from his home in Ur with his father and brother further west to the land of Canaan. Canaan you might remember is the son of Ham who was cursed for his father's sin. Canaan would later be mostly exterminated but also subjected to the Israelites, Abraham's children 400 years later in Joshua, Judges and Samuel. God gives the land of the Canaanites to Abram but it will take some time to fulfill. Just remember that when you are waiting on God.

Now the most important part of this scripture is the second half of verse3 "in you all the families of the earth shall be blessed." It is a promise to be reiterated a number of times to Abram and his family. "In you" that is in your seed (singular) all nations will be blessed. Because this seed we are told is Jesus. Jesus is the great blessing not only for the Jews and the Israelites but also for all peoples everywhere at all times and places. Jesus is the seed who opens the gate of heaven for all people, Jew and Gentile, male and female, rich, poor, slave and free.

Well you can hardly be a better blessing than that. We see the fulfillment of that as we look back over the last 2000 years since Christ ascended into heaven. Romans, Asians, the Germanic hoards, Celts, Nubians, Ethiopians, Kenyans, Indians, Chinese, Mongols, Russians, and even Australians and Kiwi's have all had the good news of the seed of Abraham, Jesus brought to them and many have come to faith to receive and believe in the blessing of the seed.

Today the blessing is brought to you. God has provided you this day a key, a ladder, and open gate to heaven. It is Jesus. Trust and believe he is your divine gift to eternal life and you will possess not just a piece of Palestine but the new heavens and the new earth, the heavenly Jerusalem.

Gracious Father, grant us such faith in your son Jesus Christ that he is the promised seed that we may possess the land promised to our father Abraham. In Jesus' name we pray, amen.

Lent day 8 Thursday
Read Mark 4:21–41
Mar 4:38-41 But he was in the stern, asleep on the cushion. And they woke him and said to him, "Teacher, do you not care that we are perishing?" (39) And he awoke and rebuked the wind and said to the sea, "Peace! Be still!" And the wind ceased, and there was a great calm. (40) He said to them, "Why are you so afraid? Have you still no faith?" (41) And they were filled with great fear and said to one another, "Who then is this, that even the wind and the sea obey him?"

You know I've been caught in a storm in the Gulf and on Lake Pontchartrain and ask God to calm things down and you know what. Nothing. I felt like the disciples at times. Lord don't you care that we are perishing?! How about you? You've ever felt as if the Lord simply isn't listening? Do you ever feel as if Jesus didn't care? Maybe something even worse, you believe Jesus wasn't able to help.

Jesus asked the disciples "Why are you so afraid? Have you still no faith?" You see fear is the opposite of faith and love. We don't always know why Jesus is letting us go through the things we go through. We may indeed fear he doesn't care or isn't able to help. But when we look at the story we see Jesus certainly able to help. How is he able to calm the wind and the seas? Who is he that he is able to do so? Very simply he is the one who created the heavens and the earth, the wind and the waves, the mountains and the deep. Having created them they are subject to him.

Well that's all very nice and good but what does that have to do with me when I'm in the troubles of life? Simply this, we are to trust Jesus no matter what. What Satan, the world, our neighbor, our enemy and even our own flesh throw at us, they are nothing compared to the incredible inheritance our Father in heaven has planned for us. We need not fear anyone or anything because Christ is on our side, he does love and care for us. But even as he has gone to the cross for us, we will share in his sufferings in this life. We must simply trust him that it's really worth it.

Lord, when crosses, trials, tribulations and troubles come upon us, grant us faith to believe you are the Lord of all and you are preparing us to bear the weight of eternal glory in and through these momentary afflictions. Amen.

Lent day 9, Friday
Read Gen 13:1–18
Gen 13:14-18 The LORD said to Abram, after Lot had separated from him, "Lift up your eyes and look from the place where you are, northward and southward and eastward and westward, (15) for all the land that you see I will give to you and to your offspring forever. (16) I will make your offspring as the dust of the earth, so that if one can count the dust of the earth, your offspring also can be counted. (17) Arise, walk through the length and the breadth of the land, for I will give it to you." (18) So Abram moved his tent and came and settled by the oaks of Mamre, which are at Hebron, and there he built an altar to the LORD.

Heb 11:8-16 By faith Abraham obeyed when he was called to go out to a place that he was to receive as an inheritance. And he went out, not knowing where he was going. (9) By faith he went to live in the land of promise, as in a foreign land, living in tents with Isaac and Jacob, heirs with him of the same promise. (10) For he was looking forward to the city that has foundations, whose designer and builder is God. (11) By faith Sarah herself received power to conceive, even when she was past the age, since she considered him faithful who had promised. (12) Therefore from one man, and him as good as dead, were born descendants as many as the stars of heaven and as many as the innumerable grains of sand by the seashore. (13) These all died in faith, not having received the things promised, but having seen them and greeted them from afar, and having acknowledged that they were strangers and exiles on the earth. (14) For people who speak thus make it clear that they are seeking a homeland. (15) If they had been thinking of that land from which they had gone out, they would have had opportunity to return. (16) But as it is, they desire a better country, that is, a heavenly one. Therefore God is not ashamed to be called their God, for he has prepared for them a city.

We believe scripture interprets scripture. Hebrews interprets Genesis. What did Abram see? Was it a piece of real estate on the east of the Mediterranean or a heavenly city? Perhaps both. One was the earnest for the other. The Lord did give to Abram's physical descendents that land, the real estate on in the Middle East. They are still in possession of it. They began to take possession of it when the Israelites crossed the Jordan. They had taken full possession of by the time of Solomon. Because of their sinfulness, the Israelites lost control of much of it and all of it at times, Abram's other children still possessed that land. He had thirteen kids you know.

And while the Israelites were like dust of the earth, they are even greater now in Christ. For in Christ, all who have faith in Christ are children of Abraham. We're in every country of the world practically representing every nation, tribe and tongue. And like Abraham we are looking to a city not made with human hands, the New Jerusalem. God has promised this to all who have faith in His Son, the seed of the Woman, the seed of Abram.

Lord Jesus Christ, give us such faith in you that like Abraham we may wait in patience to receive all that you have promised us. Amen.

Lent Day 9 Friday
Read Mark 5:1–20
Mar 5:9-10 And Jesus asked him, "What is your name?" He replied, "My name is Legion, for we are many." (10) And he begged him earnestly not to send them out of the country.

Those knowledgeable among us poo poo the thoughts of demons and demon possession. It's all in the mind they say. Just take a pill and spend a few decades on a couch. Well that may be sometimes. But there are demons and they do torture us and they do tempt us. If we give ourselves into sinful behavior they may even take up residence. I'm certain that most addictions while having a physical and mental side most certainly have a spiritual side as well. Usually one addiction leads to another as Jesus says, Mat 12:45 "Then it goes and brings with it seven other spirits more evil than itself, and they enter and dwell there, and the last state of that person is worse than the first. So also will it be with this evil generation."

When we are so blessed by Christ that he brings someone into our lives who will cast out our demons—we cannot get rid of them by our own power or strength but only by the good news of God's great love for us in Christ Jesus and the free gift of forgiveness purchased for us by him— then we must take up that gift and run with it. Our demons will plead with us not to get rid of them. They'll continue to tempt us to go back to those behaviors which invited them in. But continually look to Jesus. And having been freed by Christ from these demons do what the demoniac did, he went and told others. Nothing frees others from their own possessions than hearing the good news Jesus Christ. When tempted, find someone else and tell them what Jesus has done for you.

Dear Lord Jesus Christ, cast out all those demons from us which bind us and keep us from obeying you and loving our neighbor. Fill us with your Holy Spirit so they have no room in our hearts. Help us always to trust in you and to share you with those who are still in bondage to sin, the devil and the fear of death. Amen.

Lent day 10 Saturday
Read 15:1–21

Gen 15:5-18 And he brought him outside and said, "Look toward heaven, and number the stars, if you are able to number them." Then he said to him, "So shall your offspring be." (6) And he believed the LORD, and he counted it to him as righteousness. (7) And he said to him, "I am the LORD who brought you out from Ur of the Chaldeans to give you this land to possess." (8) But he said, "O Lord GOD, how am I to know that I shall possess it?" (9) He said to him, "Bring me a heifer three years old, a female goat three years old, a ram three years old, a turtledove, and a young pigeon." (10) And he brought him all these, cut them in half, and laid each half over against the other. But he did not cut the birds in half. (11) And when birds of prey came down on the carcasses, Abram drove them away. (12) As the sun was going down, a deep sleep fell on Abram. And behold, dreadful and great darkness fell upon him... (17) When the sun had gone down and it was dark, behold, a smoking fire pot and a flaming torch passed between these pieces. (18) On that day the LORD made a covenant with Abram…

Wow how many times does God have to remind Abram of his promise? Does he ever get it? Yeah, you think you're so good, but how often do you need to go to Church to hear God's promises so you don't sink down into despair or self-righteousness? The Lord repeated his promise to Abram and it was counted to him as righteousness. Right there then is the heart of the Gospel. God makes promises, man believes those promises, and God considers that as righteousness. That was the problem in the Garden. Man quit believing God's promises and he fell into death and darkness. When we believe the promises we are righteous again. We note that is all Abram did to be declared righteous. He believed.

But his faith did not stop there. Even though he believed, Abram wanted a sign. God told him to prepare some animals, to cut them in half. The Lord was going to cut a covenant with Abram so he could have a sign to rely on when he doubted. And the Lord appeared as a smoking fire pot and a flaming torch which passed between the pieces. So serious is God's promise to Abram he makes this covenant. If I break this promise, may what happened to these creatures happen to me. The Lord kept his promise and Israel possessed the land.

Now the Lord wants to fulfill his promise to Abram on a greater scale. So he makes Abram's seed, Jesus Christ to be the fulfillment of his covenant with Abram as the one whose seed blesses all nations. In Jesus God makes a covenant. I will forgive them their sins and remember them no more and I will put my law on their hearts. I will be their God and they will be my people. No animals this time. God himself in the flesh pours forth his blood. Jesus, the Lord, gives us a sign of the covenant. He gives us his body and blood with the bread and the wine so we may remember like Abraham God's covenant with us. As we partake of Christ's body and blood we can be certain God will keep this covenant with us.

Lord Jesus Christ, thank you for giving us this sign of the covenant with your true body and blood, crucified on the cross, shed in your passion and death, resurrected and ascended into heaven. May we with Abram be counted righteous for believing your word. Amen.

Lent Day 10 Saturday
Read Mark 5:21–43

Mar 5:34-42 And he said to her, "Daughter, your faith has made you well; go in peace, and be healed of your disease." (35) While he was still speaking, there came from the ruler's house some who said, "Your daughter is dead. Why trouble the Teacher any further?" (36) But overhearing what they said, Jesus said to the ruler of the synagogue, "Do not fear, only believe." (37) And he allowed no one to follow him except Peter and James and John the brother of James. (38) They came to the house of the ruler of the synagogue, and Jesus saw a commotion, people weeping and wailing loudly. (39) And when he had entered, he said to them, "Why are you making a commotion and weeping? The child is not dead but sleeping." (40) And they laughed at him. But he put them all outside and took the child's father and mother and those who were with him and went in where the child was. (41) Taking her by the hand he said to her, "Talitha cumi," which means, "Little girl, I say to you, arise." (42) And immediately the girl got up and began walking (for she was twelve years of age), and they were immediately overcome with amazement.

Faith in Christ is a mighty wondrous thing. A woman healed of her disease without even asking Christ to do something. She just believed if she touched the tassels of his cloak that she would be healed. Jesus tells her, "Your faith has made you well." Later he tells the ruler to not fear and only believe. Jesus raises his daughter from the dead. How many a pastor or a Christian with members diseased ridden wished they had the faith to heal them? How many times have we desired to go to a casket and say, "arise!"? Yet these are things that were given to Jesus to do to affirm his message, his ministry and his office.

We may begin to think because we do not do these things we have no faith. We pray, beg and plead to God to have things removed from us or our loved ones and…..nothing. Do we not have faith the size of a mustard seed? Well, no we don't. That's a lot of faith! We can be comforted in knowing the number of times Jesus accosted his disciples saying, "Ye of little faith."

But Jesus is not concerned so much with us today in the quantity of our faith as much as the quality of our faith. In the parable of the rich man and Lazarus Abraham tells the rich man, "If they will not listen to Moses and the prophets, they will not repent even if someone rises from the dead." You see that is the sort of faith Jesus is looking for in us today. He is looking for people who will believe, not because of miracles, simply because the Word of God, Moses, the Prophets, the Apostles writings say so. It is the sort of faith that believes that everything is restored at the resurrection. It believes that in Christ Jesus everything is made anew, even though we cannot see it sometimes. This calls for extraordinary faith, a faith that God gives us through his promises and makes us partakers of the divine nature. It is simple faith in Jesus and his work.

Lord God, heavenly Father, grant us your Holy Spirit that we may simply believe in the promises given us by your Son that we may be transformed into your children on the day of the resurrection of all flesh and live our lives today by such faith. In Jesus' name. Amen.

2nd Sunday in Lent

Read Gen 16:1–9, 15—17:22

Gen 17:1-2 When Abram was ninety-nine years old the LORD appeared to Abram and said to him, "I am God Almighty; walk before me, and be blameless, (2) that I may make my covenant between me and you, and may multiply you greatly."

Gen 17:10-11 This is my covenant, which you shall keep, between me and you and your offspring after you: Every male among you shall be circumcised. (11) You shall be circumcised in the flesh of your foreskins, and it shall be a sign of the covenant between me and you.

Abraham and his wife Sarah were as good as dead at this age. Abraham has gotten a son through his wife's made and he probably thought that was pretty good. But God called Abraham and his wife and made a covenant with them. The man and the woman are one. So God once again reaffirms his covenant with Abraham and adds a sign.

Now our translation (ESV) ends verse 2 with blameless. Many translations take the Hebrew word here and translate it perfect, blameless or upright. But the word here carries with it the meaning of completeness. To be complete before God is walk before him in faith, i.e. trusting God's promises. Such faith calls us to holy lives. But it is faith that completes a man.

The Lord God gives Abraham a sign to believe God's promise of him being the father of many nations with kings coming from his loins. The Lord gives it to him and all male descendents so their faith may be kindled regularly throughout the day. Their wives shall see it regularly too so their trust in the Lord's promise may be regularly kindled. That sign is circumcision. Every time Abraham's descendents went to the bathroom throughout the day, they could remember the Lord's promise to them and their faith could be rekindled.

Now the Lord has fulfilled that covenant in Jesus, we have new signs of the new covenant. We are baptized and whenever we clean ourselves or take a drink of water we can remember the Lord no longer counts our trespasses against us. We have the Lord's Supper so every time we gather for his meal we can remember God has promised us everlasting life in a new heavens and a new earth with resurrected bodies. Every time we see a tree or intersecting lines we can remember on the tree, the cross, our Lord Jesus Christ has won salvation for us and the world.

Heavenly Father, you made promises to Abraham and gave him and his descendents a sign that they may be strengthened in their faith. You also have made promises to us and given us the sacraments as signs that give and strengthen our faith. May we look upon them and have our faith regularly kindled that we may walk before you blameless until the coming our Lord Jesus Christ. In Jesus' name we pray. Amen.

Lent 2 Sunday
Read Mark 6:1–13
Mar 6:1-6 He went away from there and came to his hometown, and his disciples followed him. (2) And on the Sabbath he began to teach in the synagogue, and many who heard him were astonished, saying, "Where did this man get these things? What is the wisdom given to him? How are such mighty works done by his hands? (3) Is not this the carpenter, the son of Mary and brother of James and Joses and Judas and Simon? And are not his sisters here with us?" And they took offense at him. (4) And Jesus said to them, "A prophet is not without honor, except in his hometown and among his relatives and in his own household." (5) And he could do no mighty work there, except that he laid his hands on a few sick people and healed them. (6) And he marveled because of their unbelief. And he went about among the villages teaching.

For thirty years Jesus lived amongst his home town people of Nazareth and never did a single miracle. He was busy doing his trade as a carpenter. Now in the midst of his ministry he comes to teach yet he does only a few miracles there. They wonder about his teaching—which Mark never gives a full exposition. For Mark the summary of Jesus' teaching is the time is fulfilled, the kingdom of God is at hand. Repent and believe the good news. Jesus also teaches many parables. But the people of Nazareth do not believe Jesus' teaching nor do they put their trust in him.

The people of Nazareth questioned Jesus, his teaching and authority. Because they were familiar with him and his family before his ministry they treated him with contempt. So Jesus could do no mighty work there. It's not that Jesus didn't have the power to do so but the signs were not there for entertainment but to confirm the faith of those believed in him and his message.

While the people marveled at Jesus' teaching, Jesus marveled at their unbelief. It takes a pretty big action on their part to make God marvel. Several times in the gospels Jesus marvels at his own people's unbelief. Yet a couple of times Jesus marvels at the faith of a couple of gentiles. Jesus went about teaching the good news throughout the villages surrounding Nazareth.

The question for you today is, is Jesus marveling at your unbelief or is he marveling at your faith? All Jesus ever wants is for people to trust in him, his message or even just in his name. But why should we trust in Jesus, his message or his name? He gave up his life for you that you might have eternal life. His good news the reign of God is here capturing people's hearts. His name opens the doors to eternal life, the throne room of God Almighty. Faith that believes these things is greater than any other sign.

Lord Jesus Christ, grant us your Holy Spirit that we may believe in your word, receive eternal life, and turn our hearts and minds to your will. Amen.

Lent Day 11 Monday

Read Gen 18:1–15

Gen 18:13-14 The LORD said to Abraham, "Why did Sarah laugh and say, 'Shall I indeed bear a child, now that I am old?' (14) Is anything too hard for the LORD? At the appointed time I will return to you, about this time next year, and Sarah shall have a son."

Last reading God said he makes the dead alive and calls that which is not into being. Well a woman at the age of ninety has gone through menopause as our text today testifies to. She isn't having any babies. Barren by age is Sarah. But God promises a child next year. So, well who can blame her, she laughs at the promise. But God's promises are nothing to be laughed at.

Is anything too hard, too wonderful for the Lord? Another practically couple barren women once asked how they would become pregnant. One was a virgin. Her older cousin Elizabeth was well just old. But the angel Gabriel pronounced to Mary, "Nothing is impossible with God." Both of them had children, one was John the Baptist the other was Jesus. Both were children of promise and were children of the wonderful action of the Lord through the promise made Abraham and Sarah in Genesis eighteen, Isaac.

The Lord can do the impossible and does marvelous things. One of the marvelous, impossible things he does is bring us from being dead in trespasses and sins and giving us eternal life. He makes us children of God being born from above in the waters of baptism. Jesus said as much when asked by his disciples, "Who then can be saved"? Jesus replied, "With man this is impossible but with God, nothing is impossible."

You cannot save yourselves. There is nothing in you, no power or strength or will that can bring about your salvation from the kingdom of darkness to God's marvelous light. But the Lord through the promised seed of Abraham, our Lord Jesus Christ is God and Man. Jesus does the impossible. He wins eternal life for you. You were just as dead as Sarah's womb, but through the promise of Jesus life, death and resurrection, the Holy Spirit makes you alive again.

Trust that he has done this for you. Believe in the Lord Jesus Christ who does the impossible. Nothing is too hard or marvelous for him.

Heavenly Father as you have promised a child to a barren couple and through that promise you brought for Isaac, may the promise of salvation make us born from above that we may possess eternal life even now. In Jesus' name we pray. Amen.

Lent day 11 Monday
Read Mark 6:14–34
Mar 6:20 for Herod feared John, knowing that he was a righteous and holy man, and he kept him safe. When he heard him, he was greatly perplexed, and yet he heard him gladly.

Sometimes you may run into someone like Herod. Maybe you might be like Herod. Something in you wants to hear God's Word but you just can't commit yourself to it. For Herod, believing John's message from God would force him to change his life. He was living in adultery. Perhaps you're "living in sin." Of course living in sin can be more than just occurrences of a sexual nature. Perhaps it's drinking too much, depending on drugs, being lazy, keeping resentments etc. But we know deep inside should we believe God, should we believe the Word of Christ our life would change. And we would be correct.

When the Word of God has its way with us we will change. Indeed, when the Word of God does it work on us we die. We go to baptism and are buried with Christ. Death is scary. It leads to the unknown or uncertain because while we may know what awaits us, it is based on a promise. And so we are called to trust. Herod would not allow himself to die and trust God's Word.

What are you going to do today? God has promised you forgiveness, love and mercy in Christ Jesus. Will you trust this today?

Holy Spirit, grant us your favor and bring the word of promise to us. Grant us faith to believe it and covert us that we may die to self and live for Christ. Amen.

Lent day 12 Tuesday
Read Gen 21:1–21

Gen 21:17-20 And God heard the voice of the boy, and the angel of God called to Hagar from heaven and said to her, "What troubles you, Hagar? Fear not, for God has heard the voice of the boy where he is. (18) Up! Lift up the boy, and hold him fast with your hand, for I will make him into a great nation." (19) Then God opened her eyes, and she saw a well of water. And she went and filled the skin with water and gave the boy a drink. (20) And God was with the boy, and he grew up. He lived in the wilderness and became an expert with the bow.

While the promised seed is to come from Isaac, God's promise rest on all of Abraham's children. Ishmael is a child of Abraham also. Though the child of the slave woman would have no part in Isaac's inheritance, he will become a great nation because of Abraham. We will see in few chapters after Abraham's death that Ishmael has 12 children who are 12 princes. They inhabit the area opposite of Egypt to Assyria.

So God takes the boy and his mother and provides for him.

What can we learn from this? God keeps his promises. What promises has God made to you? Mat 6:33 But seek first the kingdom of God and his righteousness, and all these things will be added to you. Mat 7:7-11 "Ask, and it will be given to you; seek, and you will find; knock, and it will be opened to you. (8) For everyone who asks receives, and the one who seeks finds, and to the one who knocks it will be opened. (9) Or which one of you, if his son asks him for bread, will give him a stone? (10) Or if he asks for a fish, will give him a serpent? (11) If you then, who are evil, know how to give good gifts to your children, how much more will your Father who is in heaven give good things to those who ask him! Act 2:38-39 And Peter said to them, "Repent and be baptized every one of you in the name of Jesus Christ for the forgiveness of your sins, and you will receive the gift of the Holy Spirit. (39) For the promise is for you and for your children and for all who are far off, everyone whom the Lord our God calls to himself."

Rom 4:22-25 That is why his faith was "counted to him as righteousness." (23) But the words "it was counted to him" were not written for his sake alone, (24) but for ours also. It will be counted to us who believe in him who raised from the dead Jesus our Lord, (25) who was delivered up for our trespasses and raised for our justification. Rom 9:6-8 But it is not as though the word of God has failed. For not all who are descended from Israel belong to Israel, (7) and not all are children of Abraham because they are his offspring, but "Through Isaac shall your offspring be named." (8) This means that it is not the children of the flesh who are the children of God, but the children of the promise are counted as offspring. Gal 3:26-29 for in Christ Jesus you are all sons of God, through faith. (27) For as many of you as were baptized into Christ have put on Christ. (28) There is neither Jew nor Greek, there is neither slave nor free, there is no male and female, for you are all one in Christ Jesus. (29) And if you are Christ's, then you are Abraham's offspring, heirs according to promise.

And of course there are many more which our Lord has kept and will keep.

O Lord our God, you have made and kept so many wonderful promises. Grant us faith to believe these promises until you have fulfilled them before our very eyes. In Jesus' name. Amen.

Lent day 12 Tuesday
Read Mark 6:35–56
Mar 6:48-50 And he saw that they were making headway painfully, for the wind was against them. And about the fourth watch of the night he came to them, walking on the sea. He meant to pass by them, (49) but when they saw him walking on the sea they thought it was a ghost, and cried out, (50) for they all saw him and were terrified. But immediately he spoke to them and said, "Take heart; it is I. Do not be afraid."

The story of Jesus feeding the 5,000 and him walking on the water both teach us the same lesson. Indeed we have to wait a minute to figure what that is. But it will help us to figure out what is the question we should be asking. Well, what is that question? Give up? It is this, who is this that can feed 5,000 (not including women and children who were probably there also) with several loaves of bread and few fish and come up with leftovers AND can walk on the water?

Got any ideas? Well I'll tell who. It is I, which is the one who said "I am who I am." The Lord God Almighty in the flesh is he. He who blessed the plants and the fish and the birds and the animals and said be fruitful and multiply simply shortens the whole operation and multiplies what he has on hand. He who formed the earth from the waters with his almighty word, he's walking on the water to meet his disciples.

And how does that help us? His word, "Take heart, do not be afraid." You see God in Christ Jesus is on your side. He only wants what is best for you and whatever thinks you think that is happening to you that aren't so hot, he has the word, "He works all things for good for those who love him who have been called according to his purpose." It was when they were hungry he fed them. It was when they were in the storm, he came to him. When you are baptized Jesus calls you to be one with him and him one with you. He's your friend as now you have the faith of Abraham and Abraham was God's friend. So take heart! Don't be afraid! Jesus is on your side.

Almighty God, Heavenly Father, help us in the midst of trials and tribulations that in Christ Jesus you consider us your friends and promise to work good for us in the midst of ill. Amen.

Lent Day 13 Wednesday
Read Gen 21:1–21
Gen 21:1-6 The LORD visited Sarah as he had said, and the LORD did to Sarah as he had promised. (2) And Sarah conceived and bore Abraham a son in his old age at the time of which God had spoken to him. (3) Abraham called the name of his son who was born to him, whom Sarah bore him, Isaac. (4) And Abraham circumcised his son Isaac when he was eight days old, as God had commanded him. (5) Abraham was a hundred years old when his son Isaac was born to him. (6) And Sarah said, "God has made laughter for me; everyone who hears will laugh over me."

One promise down, more promises to come. One thing we can say about our Lord and God is he is a God of promises. Not only does the Lord make promises, he fulfills his promises. In today's lesson we are to learn that. The Lord made a promise twenty-five years ago to Abraham. He would have an heir with his wife Sarah. Now that promise is fulfilled. We should think about that as we look into the promises of God. Sometimes they are long in coming. Indeed, God had made another promise to Abraham. His descendents would inherit the land of the Canaanites.

But first Isaac was born, then Israel, then Israel's sons. Israel would have to spend another 500 years in Egypt growing into a multitude (another one of God's promises) before he brought them back to take the land.

Another 1500 years would pass until another of God's promises would come to pass. The seed through whom all nations of the world would be blessed. That promise was fulfilled in Jesus of Nazareth. In Jesus of Nazareth, the Lord God became man. Through his suffering and death peace was made between God and man. Salvation was won for all people of all places and times.

The Lord has made you a promise. If you would believe, trust in him, Jesus, that he has indeed won salvation for you, you would have eternal life. On the last day when he returns (another promise) you would be raised from the dead to eternal life. Now, it has been almost 2000 years since the Lord made that promise and it may be another 2000 before he returns. But Jesus is gathering more children for Abraham from every nation, language and tongue. From our perspective it may seem like a long time. Yet we know from past experience and evidence from Scripture, the Lord keeps his promises. You can trust him to keep this promise too.

Heavenly Father, while we may grow impatient in waiting for you to deliver on your promises, may the fulfillment of your promises past increase our faith and our patience that we may rejoice in all the family you are gathering to Abraham in your Son Jesus Christ. In Jesus' name we pray. Amen.

Lent Day 13 Wednesday
Read Mark 7:1–23
Mar 7:20-23 And he said, "What comes out of a person is what defiles him. (21) For from within, out of the heart of man, come evil thoughts, sexual immorality, theft, murder, adultery, (22) coveting, wickedness, deceit, sensuality, envy, slander, pride, foolishness. (23) All these evil things come from within, and they defile a person."

Well the good news here is eating Rib Eye on Friday even Good Friday is not a sin. Also and maybe even more important, Jesus declares Bacon to be clean. The bad news is Jesus really just cuts to the heart of the matter, our hearts. Because who among us has never thought about anything bad. Evil deeds don't make us bad; our bad hearts make us bad. The deeds are just the outward symptoms of an inward disease. St. James talks about it this way, "Jas 1:13-16 Let no one say when he is tempted, "I am being tempted by God," for God cannot be tempted with evil, and he himself tempts no one. (14) But each person is tempted when he is lured and enticed by his own desire. (15) Then desire when it has conceived gives birth to sin, and sin when it is fully grown brings forth death. (16) Do not be deceived, my beloved brothers."

There is only one hope, Jesus make us clean. John 13:10 Jesus said to him, "The one who has bathed does not need to wash, except for his feet, but is completely clean. And you are clean, but not every one of you." John 15:3 "Already you are clean because of the word that I have spoken to you." In the waters of baptism Jesus speaks his word to us and makes us clean. So there is good news and bad news. Now Jesus has given a new heart through the gift of baptism. We are made "good trees." The bad news is he left us with the old flesh. Rom 7:16-17 Now if I do what I do not want, I agree with the law, that it is good. (17) So now it is no longer I who do it, but sin that dwells within me." And so we live in a perpetual lent in this life. We are called to live lives of repentance. We confess the sin that dwells within and Jesus declares us clean. In the world to come at least, this old flesh is shed and destroyed and we get new bodies which live by the Spirit.

Father, give us continually your Holy Spirit that we may confess the sin within and be cleansed by the Word of Forgiveness from Christ Jesus, You Son. Amen.

Lent Day 14 Thursday
Read Genesis 24:1–31
Gen 24:2-5 And Abraham said to his servant, the oldest of his household, who had charge of all that he had, "Put your hand under my thigh, (3) that I may make you swear by the LORD, the God of heaven and God of the earth, that you will not take a wife for my son from the daughters of the Canaanites, among whom I dwell, (4) but will go to my country and to my kindred, and take a wife for my son Isaac." …6 Abraham said to him, "See to it that you do not take my son back there.

Why doesn't Abraham want his servant to take a wife for Isaac from among the Canaanites? Is Abraham racist, xenophobic? Not exactly. The Canaanites were of the son of Canaan whom Noah cursed. On top of that they worshipped other gods who are not gods. This often leads to the other spouse being led away from the true worship of the Lord. The Canaanites would have no part in the land that God was given to Abraham and his descendents. Indeed because of their sins, the Lord would one day use the descendants of the Abraham, the Israelites to wipe out the Canaanites and the people who lived there who worshipped other gods.

Abraham would prefer that Isaac get a wife from his own people which is why he sends his servant there. But we see that he wasn't completely opposed to a wife from somewhere else, just not from Canaan.

But there was something else. He did not want Isaac to return to his family homeland. Why was that? Because the Lord God had promised him the land where he was. If Isaac would have returned and stayed in Haran, that would be tantamount to rejecting the Lord's covenant with him.

What shall we say to this then as Christians? Perhaps one, we should not be unequally yoked to unbelievers. Marriage is a heavy yoke. If you are a Christian then if you are not married yet, do not marry an unbeliever. If you are already married pray for the conversion of your spouse and live a life worthy of a Christian. Secondly, do not return or look back at you former life with longing. If you have always been a Christian, don't look to the lives of unbelievers as something desirable, for that would be turning back on the promises the Lord has made to you, a new heavens and a new earth where righteousness reigns.

If you are not currently a believer, hear this, the Lord Jesus Christ has been given as a covenant the Lord God has made with you. On account of Christ's work the Lord no longer holds your trespasses against you. Be repentant and be baptized into the household of God, even as Abraham's servants were circumcised and you will have an inheritance as one of the people of God.

Heavenly Father, you call us to leave this world and to join ourselves with your Son Jesus Christ to gain your kingdom. Grant us such faith that we may not look back at our old lives but live joyfully in the promise of everlasting life. In Jesus' name we pray. Amen.

Lent Day 14 Thursday
Read Mark 7:24–37
Mar 7:28-29 But she answered him, "Yes, Lord; yet even the dogs under the table eat the children's crumbs." (29) And he said to her, "For this statement you may go your way; the demon has left your daughter."

This story is expanded in the other gospels. But we have this foreign woman who has not right to come to Jesus. In Matthews's gospel she does try to manipulate Jesus calling him by his Jewish titles. Jesus is not impressed and in none of the stories does Jesus act like a Jesus anyone on the street would recognize. He treats her pretty roughly. He even calls her a dog.

What you need to know is this: You have nothing on God or Jesus. You have not right to come to God or Jesus and ask him for anything. You cannot manipulate Jesus or the Father into doing your bidding. You cannot go and do good hoping God will take notice and then answer your prayers or bidding because of them.

Why does Jesus give in to this woman? Why would the Father listen to us since he owes us nothing? Jesus tells us, "For this statement." What statement was that? Acceptance of what Jesus tells her and her unrelenting faith that Jesus can and will do what she ask. Jesus calls her a dog. She says fine, even dogs get scraps, now give me a scrap. She's a pit-bull. You need to be a pit-bull when you pray to God as well. Never give up until God gives you what you ask for trusting he will do it. Do not doubt. Pit bulls don't doubt. They latch on and don't let go. Do pit-bull prayers.

Jesus, give us such faith that we like the woman may ever trust you no matter what and be impudent in our prayers. Amen.

Lent Day 15 Friday
Read Gen 24:32–52, 61–67

Gen 24:63-67 And Isaac went out to meditate in the field toward evening. And he lifted up his eyes and saw, and behold, there were camels coming. (64) And Rebekah lifted up her eyes, and when she saw Isaac, she dismounted from the camel (65) and said to the servant, "Who is that man, walking in the field to meet us?" The servant said, "It is my master." So she took her veil and covered herself. (66) And the servant told Isaac all the things that he had done. (67) Then Isaac brought her into the tent of Sarah his mother and took Rebekah, and she became his wife, and he loved her. So Isaac was comforted after his mother's death.

We might note the character of Isaac here. What is he doing? He's meditating in the evening. We should all take some time out during the day to spend time pondering and praying God's Word. Isaac is a man devoted to the Lord who has blessed his father and now is blessing him.

We note Rebekah. What is her character? What is she displaying? Modesty. Something not so clearly demonstrated by today's Christian women. Modesty just isn't for minutes before a man says, "I do." It ought to be the whole of the relationship before the wedding.

What a beautiful and simple marriage ceremony. The servant brought the woman to the man; the man takes the woman into his mother's tent and Voila! They're married. No drama.

Finally we see the most important thing. Isaac loved Rebekah! No, it wasn't a euphemism. He gave his life for her. She became a helpmeet to him. This is what marriage is supposed to be about, the husband loving the wife as Christ Jesus loved the Church. The wife being there for the husband to assist him as the Church does the work of Christ here on earth.

St. Paul describes it nicely here: Eph 5:22-27 Wives, submit to your own husbands, as to the Lord. (23) For the husband is the head of the wife even as Christ is the head of the church, his body, and is himself its Savior. (24) Now as the church submits to Christ, so also wives should submit in everything to their husbands. (25) Husbands, love your wives, as Christ loved the church and gave himself up for her, (26) that he might sanctify her, having cleansed her by the washing of water with the word, (27) so that he might present the church to himself in splendor, without spot or wrinkle or any such thing, that she might be holy and without blemish.

Lord Jesus Christ, may those who you have called into the holy vocation of marriage show the love and respect for one another as You and Your Church are reality of this institution. Amen.

Lent Day 15 Friday
Read Mark 8:1–21

Mar 8:1-9 In those days, when again a great crowd had gathered, and they had nothing to eat, he called his disciples to him and said to them, (2) "I have compassion on the crowd, because they have been with me now three days and have nothing to eat. (3) And if I send them away hungry to their homes, they will faint on the way. And some of them have come from far away." (4) And his disciples answered him, "How can one feed these people with bread here in this desolate place?" (5) And he asked them, "How many loaves do you have?" They said, "Seven."… Mar 8:15-16 And he cautioned them, saying, "Watch out; beware of the leaven of the Pharisees and the leaven of Herod." (16) And they began discussing with one another the fact that they had no bread… Mar 8:20-21 "And the seven for the four thousand, how many baskets full of broken pieces did you take up?" And they said to him, "Seven." (21) And he said to them, "Do you not yet understand?"

The Pharisees asked for a sign and Jesus says they will not get one yet Jesus before this request performs this miracle. Did they just completely miss it? Did they not hear from these four thousand people whom Jesus fed in the wilderness concerning this? I guess if you feed 4000 people with seven loaves of bread and few small fish that isn't good enough. Jesus, however, does feed the people and provide for them. His heart went out to them because they were hungry for the word and they were hungry for food. Jesus provides them with both.

Jesus warns his disciples to watch out of for the leaven of the Pharisees and Herod. They completely miss the point here as well. The leaven is their false teachings. Now not everything the Pharisees taught was false and who know what Herod was doing. But the Pharisees seemed to miss out on several things. One they prized their traditions which were made up by men to keep the law over and above the Law of Moses itself. Secondly they seemed to miss out on the grace of God. Thirdly they didn't recognize Jesus for who he is. We too need to be aware of these things in our own lives in Christ and the Church.

The disciples don't get it. They think Jesus is talking about bread and that they didn't bring any. He seems a little flabbergasted at it. If Jesus can feed 4000 people with a several loaves of bread and a couple of fish, not having food on hand is not going to be a problem with him. The question then is do we get it? Do we believe and understand Jesus is the Lord of Heaven and Earth? Do we trust him to take care of us? Do we believe Jesus is going to take not only of our spiritual needs but also our physical? Just what sort of Jesus do you worship?

Lord Jesus Christ, give us your Holy Spirit that we may believe and understand who you are and what you have done for us that we may live in true faith and love all the days of our life. Amen.

Lent Day 16 Saturday
Read Gen 27:1–29

Gen 27:28-29 May God give you of the dew of heaven and of the fatness of the earth and plenty of grain and wine. (29) Let peoples serve you, and nations bow down to you. Be lord over your brothers, and may your mother's sons bow down to you. Cursed be everyone who curses you, and blessed be everyone who blesses you!"

Reading this account and remembering all the Sunday School lessons you have probably encountered, you might think that Rebecca and Jacob were being deceitful. Well in a sense they were. They were certainly trying to deceive Isaac into giving Jacob the blessing of Isaac. Receiving a blessing was a big thing. Isaac, like his father Abraham, was a prophet of the Lord. Their blessing came with it the power to come into existence. What they blessed would come to pass. Isaac seeing his time has come had decided to bless Esau who was the oldest of the two twins and the son whom he loved.

But Isaac was acting contrary to the will of God revealed to Rebecca. It is recorded here: Gen 25:23 And the LORD said to her, "Two nations are in your womb, and two peoples from within you shall be divided; the one shall be stronger than the other, the older shall serve the younger." It was the Lord's choice that the blessing, the covenant He made with Abraham and given to Isaac to pass on to Jacob and not Esau. It was Isaac who was acting deceitfully. Rebecca and Jacob are acting in accordance with the prophetic Word of God.

Jacob was God's choice. God does seem at times to choose the least expected one to be the one through whom he will bring about his action and blessing. Abraham was an old man already when God called him. Jacob is the younger of the two twins. Judah isn't the oldest son but God chooses his tribe to be the line of the messiah. David was the youngest son whom the Lord chooses to make king of Israel. And Jesus is born of the poorest descendents of David to become the savior of the world.

And what about you? 1Co 1:27-29 "But God chose what is foolish in the world to shame the wise; God chose what is weak in the world to shame the strong; (28) God chose what is low and despised in the world, even things that are not, to bring to nothing things that are, (29) so that no human being might boast in the presence of God." We should not think the Lord chose us to have faith in Christ because we are such stellar examples of humanity. Yet that it may be by grace and not by merit we enter the kingdom of heaven, the Lord chose you to be one of his saints in glory. He chose you to receive the Holy Spirit, have faith and become a child of Abraham. How do you know he chose you? He put his name on you in baptism.

Heavenly Father, we thank and praise you for your choice that we might have faith and eternal life in your Son Jesus. Ever keep us in this faith unto life everlasting. In Jesus' name we pray. Amen.

Lent Day 16 Saturday
Read Mark 8:22–38
Mar 8:29-30 And he asked them, "But who do you say that I am?" Peter answered him, "You are the Christ." (30) And he strictly charged them to tell no one about him.

It is a theme in Mark. Jesus doesn't want to be known. After healing people he tells them to tell no one. It happened in the miracle in this section of Mark and it's happening again here when Jesus tells his disciples not to tell anyone who he is. Why is that? I think it is because he wants people to simply trust his word. That is all you and I have.

In the parable of Lazarus in the rich man we get that theme. Abraham tells the rich man, "If they won't believe Moses and the prophets they won't believe even if someone rises from the dead."

Of course we have Jesus telling his disciples what it means to be the Christ. Mar 8:31 "And he began to teach them that the Son of Man must suffer many things and be rejected by the elders and the chief priests and the scribes and be killed, and after three days rise again." Having heard this Peter rebukes Jesus and says say it isn't so and Jesus rebukes Peter back. Man's version of salvation is never what God has in mind. What God has in mind is Jesus. When you consider how you are saved is Jesus your only salvation? Do you put yourself up in any way shape or form? Is there someone or something else + Jesus? If so, those are not from the mind of God.

Jesus, remove from us all that we wish to add to your salvation and steal the glory of your work for us so we may only glorify you and in doing so glorify the Father in heaven. Amen.

3rd Sunday in Lent

Read Gen 27:30–45; 28:10–22

Gen 28:13-15 And behold, the LORD stood above it and said, "I am the LORD, the God of Abraham your father and the God of Isaac. The land on which you lie I will give to you and to your offspring. (14) Your offspring shall be like the dust of the earth, and you shall spread abroad to the west and to the east and to the north and to the south, and in you and your offspring shall all the families of the earth be blessed. (15) Behold, I am with you and will keep you wherever you go, and will bring you back to this land. For I will not leave you until I have done what I have promised you."

You would probably think that because Jacob stole by deceit Esau's blessing that the Lord would be angry with him and curse him. You would be wrong, for as we said yesterday, that blessing the Lord had already promised to Jacob. Now the Lord confirms the blessing with which Isaac blessed him. It is the same blessing the Lord had promised to his grandfather Abraham.

Now it would be 450 years or so until the Lord fulfilled his promise concerning the land upon which Jacob was lying. His family would go to Egypt, grow very numerous and eventually be delivered by the Lord and conquer the Promised Land. The Lord also makes a very great promise to Jacob who will sustain him the years to come, "I am with you and will keep you wherever you go, and will bring you back to this land. For I will not leave you until I have done what I have promised you."

Now the Lord was with Jacob in all his dealings as we shall see. He blessed him with two wives, two concubines and thirteen children not to mention servants. His physical descendants are on every continent upon which the children of men live. But Jacob also has spiritual descendents on every continent as well. These are the true Israel, those who trust in the promises of the Lord. These are the Christians to whom the same Lord who spoke to Jacob spoke to his twelve disciples and speaks to us, Mat 28:20 "…And behold, I am with you always, to the end of the age." The Lord Jesus Christ, who is Israel, God's Son, joins to himself in baptism all who will believe in him. The promise to Jacob is the promise to all his disciples and we are all Abraham's and Israel's children. We have the promise of multiplying. We have the promise of his continual presence among us. We have the promise of a new heavens and a new earth where we shall dwell always with our God and Lord. In Jesus and those who trust in him are all the nations of the earth blessed. Never doubt it.

Heavenly Father, we thank you for blessing the earth with the children of Jacob and most especially with his offspring Jesus Christ through whom all nations are blessed. We thank you for making us your children by adopting us through baptism. Help us always to keep your promises before us knowing you are Lord who keeps his promises so we may always have the presence of the Lord Jesus Christ among us. In Jesus' name we pray. Amen.

3rd Sunday in Lent
Read Mark 9:1–13
Mark 9:7 And a cloud overshadowed them, and a voice came out of the cloud, "This is my beloved Son; listen to him."

Who is this on the mountaintop with Moses and Elijah? We know it is Jesus. But Jesus is somehow different. He was transfigured, metamorphasized before their eyes to reveal his glory. Who is this? The voice from the cloud tells us. This is the very only begotten Son of God the Father. Jesus is God of God, Light of Light, Very God of Very God, one in being and substance with the Father. When we say Jesus is the Son of God, we do not mean is something less than God concerning his divinity. Jesus and the Father are One.

Because this is so, the Father tells us, "Listen to him." To listen to Jesus means more than just having sound waves vibrate against our ear drums. To listen to Jesus is first and foremost to trust him and believe what he says.

And what did Jesus say? Well you could point to all the red colored words in some bibles. You wouldn't be wrong. You could say everything from Genesis to Revelation and you wouldn't be wrong (Jesus is the Word of God.) But the one thing we may want to take note of immediately following this occurrence is Jesus tells them he must suffer and die and rise again.

How can this be? How can the one who is one with the Father much less the Messiah suffer and die? Because not only is Jesus One with the Father, he is one with us. In taking on our humanity, the Son of God became one with us. He not only took on our flesh, but he takes upon himself, our sins, our guilt and our shame. He is the fulfillment of the scapegoats in the Mosaic Law. God the Father puts our sins upon Jesus and sacrifices him on the cross. Now through faith in his blood, in this divine sacrifice, you are pronounced clean, justified, not guilty, and blameless. But are you listening? Do you trust this? If you don't trust this you are not listening to Jesus. Believe this good news! The Father has provided an atoning sacrifice for you in Christ Jesus. You are reconciled to God now.

Heavenly Father, give us ears that hear and hearts that listen and believe all the good things you have provided us in your in Son Jesus Christ. In Jesus' name we pray. Amen.

Lent Day 17 Monday
Read Gen 29:1–30

Gen 29:25-28 And in the morning, behold, it was Leah! And Jacob said to Laban, "What is this you have done to me? Did I not serve with you for Rachel? Why then have you deceived me?" … (27) Complete the week of this one, and we will give you the other also in return for serving me another seven years." (28) Jacob did so, and completed her week. Then Laban gave him his daughter Rachel to be his wife.

You may be thinking, well that's good for Jacob after deceiving his father and stealing his brother's blessing. But remember, the blessing was Jacob's to begin with as the Lord had promised. You might also be wondering about what Laban is doing. Was there some custom there at that time that the oldest had to be married first? We don't know. It certainly seems as if Laban is looking for an easy way to marry off a daughter whom he might not be able to get married easily. We do see that Laban certainly is a crafty man in all his dealings with Jacob.

But here we see how God works all things out for good for those who love him, who have been called according to his purpose. (Rom. 8) For in Laban's craftiness, the Lord is working out the blessing he gave to Abraham and to Jacob. Jacob now has two wives and their maids will be his concubines. From these four women the Lord will bestow upon Jacob twelve boys and one girl. These twelve boys will become twelve tribes who multiply in the land of Egypt whom he will bring back to take the land he promised to Abraham, Isaac and Jacob.

So what is going on in your life? Do you think the Lord is withholding his blessing from you? Do you think Jesus is not fulfilling his promises to you? You may first go back to the Scriptures and see if Jesus ever made you any such promise. But we know this, whatever promises the Lord has made, they are all yes in Jesus Christ.(2Cor. 1:20) You may think the world is acting against you as Laban was Jacob, but God is using the evil and the suffering to accomplish his good purposes and fulfilling his promises to you.

Remember also, this world is not where our treasure lies or our fulfillment. The new heavens and the new earth at the return of Christ Jesus is where we look to and have our hope in. Everything in this world is passing away. Our truest hope is not for today but the return of our Lord Jesus Christ.

Heavenly Father, even as you used crafty Laban to fulfill your purpose, may we see the fulfillment of your promise that you will work all things out for our good and to that end grant us greater faith. In Jesus' name we pray. Amen.

Lent Day 17 Monday
Read Mark 9:14–32
Mar 9:23-24 And Jesus said to him, "'If you can! All things are possible for one who believes."
(24) Immediately the father of the child cried out and said, "I believe; help my unbelief!"

You can imagine the desperation of the father in today's story. You yourself may even be experience pain in your life which is chronic. In desperation the father comes to Jesus hoping Jesus can heal his son who is possessed. There is in the father the beginning of faith, but this faith is not complete. It is not a faith that really trusts but is more of wishful thinking. Jesus reproves the man for his unbelief. It was an insurance prayer. A prayer in which there is doubt. James tells us that we shouldn't expect anything from God if we doubt.

Jesus' words are therefore given us to spur the man, and us, to true faith and greater faith. The words struck the man's heart and indeed should strike ours. How many of our prayers are nothing more than wishful thinking? How many of our prayers are insurance prayers? Do we doubt?

The father answers Jesus, "I believe; help my unbelief!" And now the spark of faith is inflamed. He does not let go of Jesus. He looks to Jesus for faith, a faith that will heal his son. He is going to the right place. Faith does not come from within. We cannot generate more faith. We must simply hear the promise of God in Christ and act on it. Faith acts, trust, believes the Word of Christ. The Holy Spirit creates faith in us through this Word. Lacking faith? Hear the Word of Christ. Faith is given through it, strengthened by it and fulfilled in and by that Word.

Lord Jesus Christ, I believe, help my unbelief. Amen.

Lent Day 18 Tuesday
Read Gen 35:1–29
Gen 35:9-12 God appeared to Jacob again, when he came from Paddan-aram, and blessed him. (10) And God said to him, "Your name is Jacob; no longer shall your name be called Jacob, but Israel shall be your name." So he called his name Israel. (11) And God said to him, "I am God Almighty: be fruitful and multiply. A nation and a company of nations shall come from you, and kings shall come from your own body. (12) The land that I gave to Abraham and Isaac I will give to you, and I will give the land to your offspring after you."

The Lord God appeared a number of times to Abraham and to Jacob. Each time, the Lord retold to them his covenantal promise. Here God even renews his naming of Jacob to Israel even as Abram became Abraham. The renaming made him a new person. We see in the New Testament. Simon becomes Peter and Saul becomes Paul. The renaming establishes a new relationship. In earlier days, a Christian's middle name, given them at baptism, was his Christian name.

The Lord renews his covenant that nations would come from Jacob and kings. The land they sojourned on would become theirs. Indeed some five hundred years later that promise would become fulfilled.

This brings us to today. People often ask, "Why do I need to go to confession so often?" "Why do we need to have the Lord's Supper so often?" "Why do I even need to God to Church?" Apparently we need to because we haven't seen or heard with our eyes and ears the Lord as Abraham and Jacob did. These two the Lord apparently felt the need for them to hear the words of the covenant he made with them numerous times. How much so we who are only given the word through the witness of men long since who have gone to be with the Lord! Jesus has only given us the witness of those who heard from those who heard, from those who heard, from those who walked and ate with Jesus and saw him raised from the dead.

It is part of our nature to need to hear God's promise of salvation and receive his gifts…often. If we did not then we would be like those Israelites who turned to other gods and trusted in them for all good things in life. We would be like them and spurn the mercy and kindness of our Savior Jesus Christ. All we need to do see those who have quit meeting together around his Word and his Sacrament to see their love of Jesus run cold.

Heavenly Father, continually provide for us the word of promise that we may be gathered around it, be changed by it, and have our faith in Christ Jesus strengthened by it so we may not lose the prize of eternal life. In Jesus' name we pray. Amen.

Lent Day 18 Tuesday
Read Mark 9:33–50
Mar 9:33-35 And they came to Capernaum. And when he was in the house he asked them, "What were you discussing on the way?" (34) But they kept silent, for on the way they had argued with one another about who was the greatest. (35) And he sat down and called the twelve. And he said to them, "If anyone would be first, he must be last of all and servant of all."

It's not our culture's understanding of greatness. Though if you read some of the get rich guru's of the 20th c. like Napoleon Hill or Dale Carnegie, they would tell you, you could get anything you want if you just get enough people what they want.

I don't think Jesus is talking about that though. He's not talking about being last for the purpose of being first. What Jesus is talking about is servant hood. And indeed, it might end up for an exalted status. St. Paul understands what Jesus is talking about when he says, Php 2:3-11 "Do nothing from rivalry or conceit, but in humility count others more significant than yourselves. (4) Let each of you look not only to his own interests, but also to the interests of others. (5) Have this mind among yourselves, which is yours in Christ Jesus, (6) who, though he was in the form of God, did not count equality with God a thing to be grasped, (7) but made himself nothing, taking the form of a servant, being born in the likeness of men. (8) And being found in human form, he humbled himself by becoming obedient to the point of death, even death on a cross. (9) Therefore God has highly exalted him and bestowed on him the name that is above every name, (10) so that at the name of Jesus every knee should bow, in heaven and on earth and under the earth, (11) and every tongue confess that Jesus Christ is Lord, to the glory of God the Father."

Here we are encouraged to humble like Jesus was and then Jesus was exalted. Jesus is our example and Jesus' humiliation is the power for us to look "to the interest of others." Not for the purpose of us getting ahead per se, but simply because we love Jesus and want to be like him.

Lord Jesus Christ, so give us your Holy Spirit that we may trust in your humiliation for our behalf that we might be exalted as sons of God and that we being sons may be like you when you walked visibly among us and serve our neighbor as you served us. Amen.

Lent Day 19 Wednesday
Read Gen 37:1–36

Gen 37:26-34 Then Judah said to his brothers, "What profit is it if we kill our brother and conceal his blood? (27) Come, let us sell him to the Ishmaelites, and let not our hand be upon him, for he is our brother, our own flesh." And his brothers listened to him. (28) Then Midianite traders passed by. And they drew Joseph up and lifted him out of the pit, and sold him to the Ishmaelites for twenty shekels of silver. They took Joseph to Egypt… (32) And they sent the robe of many colors and brought it to their father and said, "This we have found; please identify whether it is your son's robe or not." (33) And he identified it and said, "It is my son's robe. A fierce animal has devoured him. Joseph is without doubt torn to pieces." (34) Then Jacob tore his garments and put sackcloth on his loins and mourned for his son many days.

God rarely uses the best, brightness and nicest people in the world to get His work done. Indeed, you probably could not find a bigger brat in the Bible than Joseph. If you read the whole lesson you are probably reminded how God would reveal things to Joseph, in particular how He would use Joseph in the future to fulfill God's purpose and promises made to Abraham, Isaac and Jacob. But Joseph being the kind of person he was would lord such things over them and they hated him for it. Who wouldn't? Even his dad who loved him more than the others would have to think twice about him sometimes.

But God would use his bratiness to get Joseph where he needed him. It stirred up his brothers to despise him enough to want to kill him. Instead at the suggestion of Judah, they spared his life but would sell him into slavery. What a favor, right? We will see later how the Lord would use this to their benefit.

But now note how Joseph is a type of Christ. Sold for 20 shekels of silver as Jesus was betrayed for 30 he is handed over to the land of Egypt, which means misery. Jesus would experience the misery of Joseph while enslaved and in fact Jesus experienced our slavery to the fear of death, sin and the power of the devil as he underwent his innocent suffering, the shedding of his blood and ultimately death.

His righteousness which covered him was torn to pieces and stained with his blood. It was shown to the Father who declares his Son as dead. A fierce animal, Satan like a lion looking for someone to devour struck out at Jesus' heel and mortally wounded him. And as the sky grew dark on that Good Friday we see the Father mourning the death of His only begotten Son.

But Christ is also the lamb. He shed his blood for us. Our righteousness, which is but filthy rags, is now through faith in Jesus is covered with His blood and His righteousness. His blood is purifying us from our sins and His righteousness is covering us like Joseph's splendid

Lord Jesus Christ, continue to pour out your blood upon us that we might be clothed with your righteousness through your grace and faith. Amen.

Lent Day 19 Wednesday
Read Mark 10:1–12
Mar 10:6-9 But from the beginning of creation, 'God made them male and female.' (7) 'Therefore a man shall leave his father and mother and hold fast to his wife, (8) and the two shall become one flesh.' So they are no longer two but one flesh. (9) What therefore God has joined together, let not man separate."

Somewhere up there it may be possible that God has arraigned for us to have soul-mates, but nothing in the bible even intimates such a concept. So how do you know if you have the right man (if you're a woman) or woman (if you're a man)[it's a shame I have to even say that]? Well it really is quite simple. You are probably not going to like it. But here it is. When you perform whatever rite is required by your state to be married you have married the right person. At that moment God has joined you together. It reminds of Arthur looking up at Merlin in Excalibur wondering if he should eat a cookie that Guenevere gave him. Merlin answers him, "You never know until you take a bite, and then of course, it's too late."

But these words of Christ are of great benefit to those who are struggling to remain married and who may be going through tough times. Perhaps there are people tempting you to leave or just to cheat and you wonder whether or not you should stay or go. Did you make the right choice when you said yes?

Jesus answers us a definitive yes, you made the right choice. God has joined you together. You have now in marriage become one flesh. St. Paul would liken it to the way that we are one Spirit with Jesus in baptism. He is always faithful, he has said yes, he knows he made the right choice in choosing you and now you are one with him.

You might want to do some preliminary work first before you off and go marry someone. Scripture tells us to marry a fellow Christian. If your future mate isn't going to church when you meet them, there's a good chance they are not going to go after you marry them. Get to know them a while, like a year before you get serious (not engaged). Make sure your parents and family approve of them. Let's face it, if they don't like the person, perhaps they see something we don't and they will be part of your family. Don't have sex before you get married to them. There's no such thing as "how do you know if you're compatible?" If one of you is male and the other is female, you are sexually compatible.

So if you are married, rest on this promise of Jesus. God has put you together. You can work through anything if you put yesterday's lesson to work in your marriage.

Lord God heavenly Father, you put men and women together in the bonds of holy matrimony. So protect all husbands and wives in their marital vows that they may keep them. Defend them from all temptations without and within that all married couples may remain faithful and help them to live out their vocations as husbands and wives to each other that they may know your great love for us in Christ Jesus. Amen.

Lent Day 20 Thursday
Read Gen 39:1–23

en 39:11-12 But one day, when he went into the house to do his work and none of the men of the house was there in the house, (12) she caught him by his garment, saying, "Lie with me." But he left his garment in her hand and fled and got out of the house.

Gen 39:19-21 As soon as his master heard the words that his wife spoke to him, "This is the way your servant treated me," his anger was kindled. (20) And Joseph's master took him and put him into the prison, the place where the king's prisoners were confined, and he was there in prison. (21) But the LORD was with Joseph and showed him steadfast love and gave him favor in the sight of the keeper of the prison.

Joseph sure is having a rough time of it. First his brothers seek to kill him but instead sell him into slavery. While he is in slavery the Lord blesses everything he does but master's wife wants to 'lie with him' and then lies to the master about Joseph trying to take advantage of her. This lands Joseph in prison. But the Lord blesses Joseph there and causes everything he does there to succeed as well.

What should we do with this? How does it apply to our lives? Can I lie to you and tell you no matter what everything will turn out grand for you because God has a plan for you? That would be a half truth. That would do you no good. What we can see here is that God is carrying out his purposes to fulfill the promise he had made with Abraham, Isaac and Jacob. If the Lord kept his promise to them, he will keep his promises to you.

And what has Jesus promised you? Mat 28:20 "And behold, I am with you always, to the end of the age." Mar 8:35 "For whoever would save his life will lose it, but whoever loses his life for my sake and the gospel's will save it." Mat 5:3-12 "Blessed are the poor in spirit, for theirs is the kingdom of heaven. (4) "Blessed are those who mourn, for they shall be comforted. (5) "Blessed are the meek, for they shall inherit the earth. (6) "Blessed are those who hunger and thirst for righteousness, for they shall be satisfied. (7) "Blessed are the merciful, for they shall receive mercy. (8) "Blessed are the pure in heart, for they shall see God. (9) "Blessed are the peacemakers, for they shall be called sons of God. (10) "Blessed are those who are persecuted for righteousness' sake, for theirs is the kingdom of heaven. (11) "Blessed are you when others revile you and persecute you and utter all kinds of evil against you falsely on my account. (12) Rejoice and be glad, for your reward is great in heaven, for so they persecuted the prophets who were before you.

With such great and wonderful promises, we shall endure all things, all tribulations, sufferings and persecutions and trials of life, knowing our Lord endured such things and will give us all things at the resurrection, most importantly his very self.

Heavenly Father, grant us your grace to endure all things for Christ' sake having your promise of eternal life for all you place their trust in your son Jesus. In Jesus' name we pray. Amen.

Lent Day 20 Thursday
Read Mark 10:13–31
Mar 10:25-27 It is easier for a camel to go through the eye of a needle than for a rich person to enter the kingdom of God." (26) And they were exceedingly astonished, and said to him, "Then who can be saved?" (27) Jesus looked at them and said, "With man it is impossible, but not with God. For all things are possible with God."

In this section Jesus is turning everything upside down. We want people to grow up so they can make up their own minds about following Jesus, Jesus tells us we must grow down and be like infants. If you want to do something to inherit eternal life, you can't just be good enough, you have to be perfect. And now in these verses Jesus is telling us it isn't those who seem to have everything in life who will enter the kingdom of God. So pointed is Jesus in his remarks here that even the disciples finally understand one most certain point that we all must first get if we are going to be saved; if the people who we think should get to heaven because they are so good and are blessed by God with earthly possessions can't get to heaven, the rest of us are in bad shape. In fact the disciples have it right here, "who can be saved."

Jesus tells us with man it is impossible. Get that. If you are a human being there is nothing you can do to be saved, at all. Nothing, zilch, nada, rien. It is IMPOSSIBLE for you do ANYTHING to be saved.

But with God all things are possible. This should bring forth a couple of other impossible things God has done in the past. The first was having Abraham who was 100 and Sarah who was 90 begets, conceived and gives birth to a healthy baby boy. The other was similar; a virgin conceived (w/o any human intermediary) and gave birth to Jesus. Now a third, that son of the Virgin is God made man. He takes our sins upon himself. He conquers sin, death and the power of the devil. He dies and rises to life again after three days in the grave never to die again.

If you believe this, you have received the gift of life, the Holy Spirit and will never die but enter into eternal life. You have passed through the eye of needle. It's impossible that man can do anything to be saved. With the God-Man and only with him, i.e. Jesus, you are saved.

Lord give us such faith that believe Jesus has done everything necessary for us to inherit eternal life, though Jesus Christ your Son our Lord, who lives and reigns with you and the Holy Spirit. Amen.

Lent Day 21 Friday
Read Gen 40:1–23
Gen 40:6-8 When Joseph came to them in the morning, he saw that they were troubled. (7) So he asked Pharaoh's officers who were with him in custody in his master's house, "Why are your faces downcast today?" (8) They said to him, "We have had dreams, and there is no one to interpret them." And Joseph said to them, "Do not interpretations belong to God? Please tell them to me."

It's interesting that God is not totally against divination. He gives the Israelites a means of divination in Exodus. It was His appointed method though that was only approved. The family of Abraham was prophets of the Most High though. He would reveal to them things happening and things to happen. Here we see Joseph has a gift to be able to interpret dreams. He attributes this gift to God.

Now this is all part of God's major plan. God uses everything at his disposal to accomplish His purposes. He actually uses Joseph's bratiness to get him to Egypt. He uses the evil mind of his brothers to get him to Egypt. Yesterday he uses the wickedness of Joseph's master's wife to get him put in prison. Now in prison, Joseph is going to meet up with someone who will be able to introduce him to Pharaoh.

You see you just never know what God is working out in your life and to what purpose. Even now in the account of Joseph we do not yet see the full purpose of God's plan. You may indeed never know the full purpose of God's plan in your life. You may never know how he may use your good character or your bad character, your good choices or your bad choices to accomplish something He wants to accomplish.

Where you want to be though is in God's good favor. How do you end up there? By His grace of course! Rom 8:28 "And we know that for those who love God all things work together for good, for those who are called according to his purpose." He works all things for good for those who love Him? Who is that? Those who are called according to His purpose. Who is that? How do you know you were called by God? That's simple. You know you were called to love God and be those who all things work for good by being baptized into Christ. In baptism you are joined to Christ and to His body. Christ is the beloved of the Father. In him you are beloved as well.

Lord Jesus Christ, help us to trust in work of the Father even when we cannot see what you are planning for us in our lives. May we always, in You. be in your Father's graces and have everything in our life work toward our good and the good of your Church. Amen.

Lent Day 21 Friday
Read Mark 10:32–52

Mar 10:32-40 And they were on the road, going up to Jerusalem, and Jesus was walking ahead of them. And they were amazed, and those who followed were afraid. And taking the twelve again, he began to tell them what was to happen to him, (33) saying, "See, we are going up to Jerusalem, and the Son of Man will be delivered over to the chief priests and the scribes, and they will condemn him to death and deliver him over to the Gentiles. (34) And they will mock him and spit on him, and flog him and kill him. And after three days he will rise." (35) And James and John, the sons of Zebedee, came up to him and said to him, "Teacher, we want you to do for us whatever we ask of you." (36) And he said to them, "What do you want me to do for you?" (37) And they said to him, "Grant us to sit, one at your right hand and one at your left, in your glory." (38) Jesus said to them, "You do not know what you are asking. Are you able to drink the cup that I drink, or to be baptized with the baptism with which I am baptized?" (39) And they said to him, "We are able." And Jesus said to them, "The cup that I drink you will drink, and with the baptism with which I am baptized, you will be baptized, (40) but to sit at my right hand or at my left is not mine to grant, but it is for those for whom it has been prepared."

Jesus for the 3rd time is preparing his disciples for what is to come. Certainly it was probably a drag on the disciples to hear Jesus to be speaking about his death. It seems they completely ignore his message that on the 3rd day he would rise again. Certainly while they were afraid Jesus was telling them this so they could have hope.

Jesus' word is fulfilled on Easter morning as he rises victoriously from the dead. Had the disciples paid better attention and believe the word of Jesus they would not have been in the despair they were in after his arrest and crucifixion. Jesus has also told us that we shall enter the kingdom of God through much tribulation. It should not be a surprise to us when all sorts of bad things happen to us even though we are doing everything right. But our hope is not in or of this world. Our citizenship is in heaven and our treasure is located there as well. Our hope is for the resurrection of our bodies in a new heavens and a new earth where righteousness reigns. It is these promises that keep us going when others may go into despair.

James and John perhaps completely ignored the word of Jesus about his upcoming crucifixion. They desire to sit at Jesus' left and right when he comes into his glory. But those places have been picked already by the Father. Jesus comes into his glory not with bright lights and cheers of hosannas. Jesus comes into his glory when he is crucified. Jesus' glory is best seen as he wins mercy, life, salvation and forgiveness, as he is crucified on the cross. The thieves on his right and on his left are those who have been appointed. One has faith unto eternal life and one disbelieves and gains eternal death.

Our lives as Christians are not ones of victory after victory in life but of suffering, persecution, and hardships as we participate in the sufferings of Christ. But these things are preparing us to bear the weight of eternal glory when Christ returns.

Lord Jesus Christ, even as you have suffered as you entered your glory you have set us who follow you to bear our crosses. Grant us faith in you and your promise of eternal glory if we remain faithful unto death and thank you for the gift of perseverance. Amen.

Lent Day 22 Saturday
Read Gen 41:1–27
Gen 41:28-32 It is as I told Pharaoh; God has shown to Pharaoh what he is about to do. (29) There will come seven years of great plenty throughout all the land of Egypt, (30) but after them there will arise seven years of famine, and all the plenty will be forgotten in the land of Egypt. The famine will consume the land, (31) and the plenty will be unknown in the land by reason of the famine that will follow, for it will be very severe. (32) And the doubling of Pharaoh's dream means that the thing is fixed by God, and God will shortly bring it about…

There are a couple of ways one could take this. When I read it I sometimes wonder, why do seven good years and seven years of famine at all? I mean, you're God. Just have everything nice the whole time. From this fallen person's point of view, it sometimes just makes me wonder. But God has a plan.

He had told Abraham his descendents would go down to Egypt and stay there 4oo years, enter into hard labor and then be delivered to the promised land of Canaan. Again, God just doesn't do things the way I would have. But if you ever watched "Bruce Almighty" you'll understand why God has not put me in charge. It really helps to have omniscience along with omnipotence, all wisdom and have it ruled by grace, mercy, and loving-kindness.

So, the plenty will feed the famine. The famine will bring the family of Joseph to Egypt to fulfill God's purposes.

Do you find yourself wondering why on earth God is doing the things he is doing in your life? Why doesn't he just zap us and make all things good? Why does he make it so hard and complicated all the time? Perhaps God isn't simple as the Greeks think but he is particularly complicated at least to fallen man. Our minds simply cannot wrap themselves around the mind of God. But this should not surprise us. Isa 55:8-9 For my thoughts are not your thoughts, neither are your ways my ways, declares the LORD. (9) For as the heavens are higher than the earth, so are my ways higher than your ways and my thoughts than your thoughts.

Yet the one thing we can see here is that God is determined to let his people know what is going to happen. We may not always know why things happen but the Lord has let us know a lot of what will happen. At least he has let us know the most important things we need to know for today. Our everyday workings in the faith of Jesus, well, they work into his plans for you and for the good of the Church. Sometimes it's not really about you. God may not be keeping you around because you have something left to do, sometimes he may have something left to be done to or for you. Sometimes it has nothing to do with you directly. This calls us to trust simply in God's good kindness towards us in Christ Jesus.

Lord Jesus Christ, you revealed to Pharaoh what was going to happen to place Joseph in a position of power to save your chosen people. Help us at times to get a glimpse of what you have planned for us and faith to trust you know what you're doing when you keep it to yourself. Amen.

Lent Day 22 Saturday
Read Mark 11:1–19

Mar 11:15-17 and they came to Jerusalem. And he entered the temple and began to drive out those who sold and those who bought in the temple, and he overturned the tables of the money-changers and the seats of those who sold pigeons. (16) And he would not allow anyone to carry anything through the temple. (17) And he was teaching them and saying to them, "Is it not written, 'My house shall be called a house of prayer for all the nations'? But you have made it a den of robbers."

Should you become a Christian later in life you'll probably experience this more graphically than those brought in as infants. It can even happen if you fall away and then later come back to faith in Jesus. (Now don't go and fall away just so you see what I mean). But even those brought into the faith as events still experience this, it's just that they are so used to it; it doesn't affect them as dramatically. They simply are more mature and have had those spiritual muscles built up. It just isn't as much work for them.

Now you are probably wondering what I am talking about. It's about cleaning house. When Jesus comes and makes your body, you heart, mind and soul his temple, he is not at all like me when I clean house. I'm a piler, not quite a hoarder. I keep thinking I'll use that someday, probably the day after I throw it away. But Jesus isn't like that at all. Everything has to go. Most of our cherished possessions of spirit, soul, mind and sometimes even physical possessions must go. They are idols of the heart that can try to steal us away again from love of the Father and the love of the Son.

We are meant to be houses of prayer; prayer for ourselves and prayer for others most importantly. Our hearts are temples where the sacrifices of praise and thanksgiving are continually being lifted up. But that can't happen while we are still thinking God is working on a currency exchange program. Nope. God is on the gift giving program. He gives us eternal life, forgiveness, his righteousness, his holiness all for free in Jesus. Jesus has to make room and when you believe Jesus gives us these things for free, guess what? Jesus starts making room. So don't fear too much when you find yourself having to get rid of a whole lot of your former or present life when Jesus moves in. He is replacing it all with much better stuff.

Dear Jesus, help me not to resist when you start you house cleaning project in me, but let me realize all you're replacing it with and give me a heart of thanks and praise. Amen.

4th Sunday in Lent

Read Gen 41:28–57

Gen 41:38-41 And Pharaoh said to his servants, "Can we find a man like this, in whom is the Spirit of God?" (39) Then Pharaoh said to Joseph, "Since God has shown you all this, there is none so discerning and wise as you are. (40) You shall be over my house, and all my people shall order themselves as you command. Only as regards the throne will I be greater than you." (41) And Pharaoh said to Joseph, "See, I have set you over all the land of Egypt."

Can you imagine that? Joseph, sold into slavery by his brothers, sent to prison by his master, is now master over all Egypt. This might not be something that will happen to you in your lifetime. It may be hard for you to figure out how this may apply to your life. But it does. For even if the Lord doesn't make you master over all you see, he does raise up rulers from among the people to do his will. Paul reminds of that in Romans, Rom 13:1 "Let every person be subject to the governing authorities. For there is no authority except from God, and those that exist have been instituted by God."

God does have a plan for your life and he has promised he cares for you. But not everybody can be king in this life in this age. Yet you are individually important in his plans. There is no one who is not necessary. We cannot always see it and it may not always be made manifest in our lives. We all have our parts to play. Joseph's brothers and Joseph's master and his master's wife all had a part to play in putting Joseph in power to accomplish God's will.

Hopefully, you as Christians will not be playing the part of Joseph's brothers or Potipher's adulterous wife. We should be confident though that God is raising people to positions of power for his good purposes, for the good of the Church and the spreading of the Gospel of Jesus Christ. We should be humble to take the lots in life God places before us and do everything he has given us to do to the glory of Jesus.

Even if we are not raised to greatness in the eyes of the world we should remember, 1Pe 2:9 "But you are a chosen race, a royal priesthood, a holy nation, a people for his own possession, that you may proclaim the Excellencies of him who called you out of darkness into his marvelous light." We are children, through baptism, of the King of all creation, brothers and sisters of the King of Kings and Lord of Lords. And on the last day if we are faithful Jesus will place us on his Father's throne.

Heavenly Father, ever give us faith in your divine providence that we may live in peace and quietness all our days no matter what callings you have called us to, knowing your plan for us and your Church shall prevail. In Jesus' name we pray. Amen.

4th Sunday in Lent
Read Mark 11:20–33
Mar 11:21-25 And Peter remembered and said to him, "Rabbi, look! The fig tree that you cursed has withered." (22) And Jesus answered them, "Have faith in God. (23) Truly, I say to you, whoever says to this mountain, 'Be taken up and thrown into the sea,' and does not doubt in his heart, but believes that what he says will come to pass, it will be done for him. (24) Therefore I tell you, whatever you ask in prayer, believe that you have received it, and it will be yours. (25) And whenever you stand praying, forgive, if you have anything against anyone, so that your Father also who is in heaven may forgive you your trespasses."

All I have to say is this: Our prayers are full of doubt and uncertainty and are most certainly sinful because the lack of faith in which they are prayed. Seriously, we have a promise from the Lord Jesus Christ here. Who among us prays like this? Perhaps the 2 or 5 yr. old among us prays with such faith.

But the good thing is we have a promise. If we pray for something and do not doubt in our heart but believes what we say will come to pass, it will be done for us. Whatever you ask for in prayer believe you have received it [already] it will be yours. If not for anything else this would be a great incentive for us to pray our hearts out. We have an unbelievable promise from Jesus. And that is the problem. We believe that it is unbelievable. James tells us if we doubt, we should not think we will get anything from God.

We have much unbelief to be repentant of don't we. One more piece of good news, the faith required of by Jesus for answering these prayers is not the same faith required to be saved. There is saving faith and there is a gift of faith that moves mountains. The faith Jesus is talking about is the faith that moves mountains. It's not that far removed from faith in Christ to save us. In fact both are impossible for man. It is God's gift that we have faith in Christ to save us and it is also God's gift that we have such faith that moves mountains. But don't doubt your salvation if you lay your hands on your blown tire on the side of the road and it isn't fixed.

Lord Jesus Christ you have given us a great promise concerning prayer. Grant us such faith that we may move mountains if we need to. Amen.

Lent Day 23 Monday
Read Gen 42:1–38

Gen 42:17-24 And he put them all together in custody for three days. (18) On the third day Joseph said to them, "Do this and you will live, for I fear God: (19) if you are honest men, let one of your brothers remain confined where you are in custody, and let the rest go and carry grain for the famine of your households, (20) and bring your youngest brother me. So your words will be verified, and you shall not die." And they did so. (21) Then they said to one another, "In truth we are guilty concerning our brother, in that we saw the distress of his soul, when he begged us and we did not listen. That is why this distress has come upon us." (22) And Reuben answered them, "Did I not tell you not to sin against the boy? But you did not listen. So now there comes a reckoning for his blood." (23) They did not know that Joseph understood them, for there was an interpreter between them. (24) Then he turned away from them and wept. And he returned to them and spoke to them. And he took Simeon from them and bound him before their eyes.

It sure seems like Joseph is giving his brothers who represent Israel a hard time. But one can truly say they deserve it. Indeed they themselves confess such at this time. What they had done to Joseph they fear has come back upon them. At least now they confess their guilt. The fact that they do it despite the fact that Joseph is right there listening to them and they don't know shows the sincerity of their confession.

Joseph's heart had also changed during this time. While the Scriptures never say it, it is likely that he held some sort of grudge against them and certainly at the very least a few hard feelings. But their confession of their sins breaks his heart and turns to weeping. His testing of their character is showing them to be different people than they were when they sold into slavery. But Joseph still wants to test their character. He's making leave one behind and to bring the youngest, his full brother to him. There are two reasons for this. One is to see whether or not they will actually come back for the brother or leave him to rot in Egypt. The other is to see whether or not they are telling the truth about his younger brother. On top of both of those it is his intention to get the whole family in Egypt where he can save them from the famine.

Now the brothers represent Israel. Israel is a type, a representative of Christ Jesus. Note what happens at the beginning of the chapter. Israel is cast into the custody of the Egyptian for three days and on the third day he is raised from the prison. In like manner the fulfillment of Israel, Jesus Christ is buried in death and on the third day rose from the dead. In like manner Jesus departs and returns to the Father. And in like manner as Israel returns for the brother still in custody of Egypt, Jesus shall return for all his brothers still in custody of their graves and restore them to life. Jesus is the fulfillment of this passage that you may know what happened here in the life of Israel it will be fulfilled in your life. As even as Jesus is raised from the dead, all who trust in him will be raised to everlasting life.

Lord Jesus Christ, grant us such faith in your resurrection that we too shall be freed from the prison of death when you return to us with the Father and enter into eternal life in new heavens and new earth. Amen.

Lent Day 23 Monday
Read Mark 12:1–12
Mar 12:9-11 What will the owner of the vineyard do? He will come and destroy the tenants and give the vineyard to others. (10) have you not read this Scripture: "'The stone that the builders rejected has become the cornerstone; (11) this was the Lord's doing, and it is marvelous in our eyes'?"

While Jesus immediately spoke this parable to the Jews, no doubt it applies to us as well. But first we must understand how it applies to the Jews. God has called the Israelites out of Egypt to make them his own people. However over time the Israelites rebelled against God and worshipped other gods besides the Lord, sometimes alongside the Lord.

The Lord desiring the repentance of his people sent them prophets to call them back to their first love, to reject the other gods of the nations around them and to love him only. But these they either ignored, beaten or even killed at times.

Finally, the Lord sent his son Jesus Christ. They took him, insulted him, mistreated him, beat him, whipped him and finally crucified him. They were wanted what God had promised on their own terms. For this, when they did not repent of this sin, were destroyed 40 years later by the Romans.

Today, the Lord Jesus Christ has gathered a people to himself through the Word and the Holy Spirit. His people also rebel against God sometimes. They want to worship God and serve him on their own terms. God in love sends pastors to call them back to repentance, sometimes he even sends spiritual leaders among us to call back to repentance. Will we listen?

Sometimes Jesus' people mistreat and even attempt to murder by withholding wages that are truly due, even chasing them out of the place which Jesus has placed them. If God destroyed Jerusalem and the Jews for what they did in the past in ignorance what do you think he will do to those who had been born of the Spirit and act this way? If a pastor is speaking God's Word then due obedience is called for. We are rebelling against God and not a man.

Lord Jesus Christ, who has sent the prophet, who came yourself, who sends us men to call us to repentance and believe the Gospel, grant us your Holy Spirit always that we may always recognize your voice, trust you and listen to those who you send to us. Amen.

Lent Day 24 Tuesday
Read Gen 43:1–28

Gen 43:8-9 And Judah said to Israel his father, "Send the boy with me, and we will arise and go, that we may live and not die, both we and you and also our little ones. (9) I will be a pledge of his safety. From my hand you shall require him. If I do not bring him back to you and set him before you, then let me bear the blame forever.

Now Judah places his own life as a pledge for his brother Benjamin. They had to go back to Egypt to buy food. There was no way to go back without him. Benjamin, as far as Jacob is concerned is the last son of his wife Rachel. We must remember it was Judah who kept his brothers (minus Reuben) from killing Joseph. Instead, Gen 37:26 "... Judah said to his brothers, "What profit is it if we kill our brother and conceal his blood?" Now what profit are Judah and his brothers getting? But Judah is willing to risk losing Benjamin as the risk of his own life.

From Judah comes the one who puts down his own life for a pledge again for his brothers. That one from Judah is Jesus and we are his brothers. As Judah went back to Egypt (the land of misery) with his own life as a pledge to his father in order save the lives of his family, so too, Jesus comes to world (a land of misery) with his life as a pledge to the Father in order to save the lives of the human race.

Jesus comes with his lifeblood as the ransom to save us from eternal death. If we are to live and partake of eternal life then he must give his life as a pledge on the cross. And there on the cross indeed his life is required of him. By his death he has conquered Death. His death becomes our own death and we need not experience it anymore. For Jesus did not stay dead. He conquered stay dead. He rose again. Now he offers eternal life for all who put their trust, their faith in him, his name and in his works. All who have their faith in him possess eternal life now. They never taste death. They are freed from the land of misery and enter the Promised Land.

Heavenly Father, grant us such faith in Jesus, our ransom from death, that we may be freed from eternal death and possess eternal life and for all eternity in your kingdom. In Jesus' name we pray. Amen.

Lent Day 24 Tuesday
Read Mark 12:13–27

Mar 12:24-27 Jesus said to them, "Is this not the reason you are wrong, because you know neither the Scriptures nor the power of God? (25) For when they rise from the dead, they neither marry nor are given in marriage, but are like angels in heaven. (26) And as for the dead being raised, have you not read in the book of Moses, in the passage about the bush, how God spoke to him, saying, 'I am the God of Abraham, and the God of Isaac, and the God of Jacob'? (27) He is not God of the dead, but of the living. You are quite wrong."

There are two misconceptions that people have that Jesus is correcting and one that is cause by this lesson. We'll take on of first ones corrected and one cause by it together. First, much to the chagrin of many couples who are waiting to be reunited with their spouses in eternity, you won't have the status of married at the resurrection. That order of things is done away with. Will you know your spouse(s) in the world to come? Sure, but they won't be your spouse. They'll just be Bob, Sue, Kate or Tom.

Secondly, we don't become angels. The point of comparison is that angels don't marry. In the resurrection of the body, like the angels, we won't marry. Jesus came not only to redeem our souls/spirits but also to redeem our bodies. Jesus rose with his body. You're going to rise with yours. As Job says, "With my own eyes and in my own flesh I will see my Redeemer."

Thirdly, if you are Christian, you don't die. Sure your body may experience death, but you died back when you were baptized. You died with Christ. Your spirit which was dead previously was raised to life. That's why Abraham, Isaac and Jacob weren't dead when Jesus was talking to them. They were Christians. They believe in the one who would come from their loins who would save all humanity through his death.

The day Adam and Eve ate the fruit they died. Not physically, though that process began. They died spiritually. So St. Paul says we were dead in our trespasses and sins. Your unbelieving neighbors already are zombies; they're just not of the human flesh eating kind. But Baptism into Christ Jesus cures them, because Baptism gives us faith in Christ and the Holy Spirit. And that is eternal life. If you have eternal life you can't die. So Jesus says to his favorite two sisters (not his biological sisters, just two sisters who happen to be his favorites) If you die and believe in me you will live, in fact if you believe in me you will never die.

That really helps us make sense of that passage in the Creed when it says Jesus comes again to judge the living and the dead. Why judge dead people? What good would it do? Instead we should understand it as saying the believers and the unbelievers as both are raised from the dust on the last day. So are you alive or are you a zombie. If you are a zombie we have a cure: You have been saved from death by Christ Jesus' death. Believe this and you are cured.

Lord, help us ever to believe that to have faith in you means we have eternal life and let us be living when you return for us. Amen.

Lent Day 25 Wednesday
Read Gen 44:1–18, 32–34

Genesis 44:9 Whichever of your servants is found with it shall die, and we also will be my lord's servants." 10 He said, "Let it be as you say: he who is found with it shall be my servant, and the rest of you shall be innocent." 11 Then each man quickly lowered his sack to the ground, and each man opened his sack. 12 And he searched, beginning with the eldest and ending with the youngest. And the cup was found in Benjamin's sack. 13 Then they tore their clothes, and every man loaded his donkey, and they returned to the city. 14 When Judah and his brothers came to Joseph's house, he was still there. They fell before him to the ground. 15 Joseph said to them, "What deed is this that you have done? Do you not know that a man like me can indeed practice divination?" 16 And Judah said, "What shall we say to my lord? What shall we speak? Or how can we clear ourselves? God has found out the guilt of your servants; behold, we are my lord's servants, both we and he also in whose hand the cup has been found." 17 But he said, "Far be it from me that I should do so! Only the man in whose hand the cup was found shall be my servant. But as for you, go up in peace to your father."…32 For your servant became a pledge of safety for the boy to my father, saying, 'If I do not bring him back to you, then I shall bear the blame before my father all my life.' 33 Now therefore, please let your servant remain instead of the boy as a servant to my lord, and let the boy go back with his brothers. 34 For how can I go back to my father if the boy is not with me? I fear to see the evil that would find my father."

Joseph again tests his brothers. He wants to see whether or not they have changed. He wants to know whether or not they have repented of their treatment of him in wanting to kill him and selling him into slavery.

We see here they tear their clothes. It is a sign of repentance. They believe God is bringing this upon them because of what they had done to their brother Joseph. We might take a brief note to remember these are God's people. Judgment begins with the house of God. God may indeed discipline those who have been called to be his through various and sundry punishments until such time they repent. Jesus is apt to teach us, "Unless you repent you will likewise perish." Joseph uses their words against them when he searches for the cup and lays the blame squarely on the one who has it, the one he is framing, his little brother. How do his brothers act? What is their response to being sent away without Benjamin? Judah as we recall from yesterday fulfills his promise. He will stand in the place of Benjamin. He will be the substitute.

The seed of Judah, Jesus of Nazareth is our substitute so we may return home to the Father. Satan wishes to accuse us, rightly and wrongly before God. But Jesus is our scapegoat. He takes the blame. He is punished for our transgression so we may live and return to our Father in heaven without sin, guile, blame, shame or guilt. It is all laid on our elder brother Jesus.

Lord Jesus Christ, we thank you for fulfilling the promises you made in the Old Testament. Grant us faith to believe it. Amen.

Lent Day 25 Wednesday
Read Mark 12:28–44

Mar 12:41-44 And he sat down opposite the treasury and watched the people putting money into the offering box. Many rich people put in large sums. (42) And a poor widow came and put in two small copper coins, which make a penny. (43) And he called his disciples to him and said to them, "Truly, I say to you, this poor widow has put in more than all those who are contributing to the offering box. (44) For they all contributed out of their abundance, but she out of her poverty has put in everything she had, all she had to live on."

Believe it or not this connects with what today's passage starts with, "Love the Lord your God with all your heart, soul, mind and strength. Vs. 41-44 is the New Testament giving program. In the Old Testament God only required a tenth of everything, and the first born as well. But it wasn't everything. But in the New Testament God requires everything. We see this born out in the beginning of Acts where all the disciples sold everything they had and brought it to the disciples to be used as a common treasury.

The number ten represents completeness. One tenth, the tithe, represented giving God everything. It recognized that everything came from Him. However as St. Augustine once noted, "Even unbelieving Jews give ten percent. Certainly Christians can do better than unbelieving Jews."

Does this mean we have to do likewise? No. But it does mean we need to be prepared to do it. As the disciples told the men who had the donkey, "The Lord has need of it." And when the Lord has need of something we have, we need to have no attachment to it. We need to recognize everything we have it from God and for His purposes.

When we make offerings to God though, in reality, it isn't as if God really needs it. God could place whatever wealth is needed anywhere He wants. But He knows we need to know that the things we call wealth in life are not life itself. Only God is life. All life subsists and consists of Him. When we make and offering to God we are telling Him that we trust Him to take care of us. When we trust in God to take care of us we also love Him.

And God gives us the greatest reason in the world to dedicate everything to Him; He has dedicated everything to us in His Son Jesus.

Heavenly Father, help us to fear, love and trust in you above all things that we might not fear not having whatever it is we thing we need. Amen.

Lent Day 26 Thursday
Read Gen 45:1–20, 24–28
Gen 45:4-8 So Joseph said to his brothers, "Come near to me, please." And they came near. And he said, "I am your brother, Joseph, whom you sold into Egypt. (5) And now do not be distressed or angry with yourselves because you sold me here, for God sent me before you to preserve life. (6) For the famine has been in the land these two years, and there are yet five years in which there will be neither plowing nor harvest. (7) And God sent me before you to preserve for you a remnant on earth, and to keep alive for you many survivors. (8) So it was not you who sent me here, but God. He has made me a father to Pharaoh and lord of all his house and ruler over all the land of Egypt.

You just never know how God is going to turn your life around. Whether you have done evil or have been the victim of it, it is all in God's hands. It is in God's hands for God's purposes. That can be a scary thing or a good thing depending on your view of your relationship with God.

Joseph's brothers until they get the view the plan at hindsight see their evil now as a good thing or rather how God has turned it into a good thing. You rarely want to be the one perpetrating the evil in the normal scheme of thing, just in case you're wondering, just look ahead to the next book in the Bible to what happens to Pharaoh. But for God's people in Christ Jesus it all pans out.

We have the promise, Rom 8:28 "And we know that for those who love God all things work together for good, for those who are called according to his purpose." And how do we know we have been called according to his purpose? By his choosing. How do you know you are chosen? By the rite of baptism. In Baptism, you know God has placed his name, the Father, the Son and the Holy Spirit on you. There he has placed you into his Son, Jesus. Rom. 6:3ff

If you are in Christ then all things are working out for your good and the good of His Church. We don't always see it at times. It may take 450-2000 years (just read the Bible history from Israel's entrance to Egypt to the crucifixion of Jesus) but the good that God intends will not be frustrated. I think this is because despite the bad guy's line in every good movie, "You can't exist without me!" they have it backwards. Evil cannot exist without good because evil is just a perversion of the good like rust on a nail. The nail is perfectly happy and can exist without the rust. Whatever evil there is it depends upon goodness for its existence. God being the ultimate good simply removes the evil from that which being perverted and Voila! The good that was supposed to be there is there. But Tarnex won't do the job. It takes the blood of Jesus and the cross to remove it.

Lord grant us faith to believe that while we cannot see the good you are going to work from evil or good, that you will indeed keep your promise to work all things together for our good. In Jesus' name we pray, Amen.

Lent Day 26 Thursday
Read Mark 13:1–23
Mar 13:20 And if the Lord had not cut short the days, no human being would be saved. But for the sake of the elect, whom he chose, he shortened the days.

A lot of people are confused about this section of Mark and the parallel passages in the other synoptic gospels. Part of the reason they are confused is they don't recognize Jesus doesn't always answer the question his disciples asked him but the one they should have asked him. The other problem is that in the middle of his answer, Jesus does actually answer the question they asked and then continues with his other question.

But the verse above is written for our comfort. I meet so many Christians that are afraid of the end of the world. It shouldn't be so. We're supposed to be expecting it. Also Jesus teaches us in this text that being his disciple will not always be easy. You may even have to give up all you have even your very life to be a disciple of Jesus Christ.

The good news here is that Jesus cuts the time short that we have to experience the great tribulation. He tells us if he didn't, no one would be saved. But for the elect he cuts the days short. Now just who are the elect and where can you find them? How do you know if you are one of the elect?

We know God chose us in Christ Jesus before the foundation of the world. (Eph. 1) Now where in our life do we know we are in Christ Jesus? Well let's back up a little. First we must know that no one is justified in God's sight based on what they have done. (Rom. 3) Secondly we know God so loved the world he sent his son to be the atoning sacrifice for the world. He sent Jesus into the world not to condemn it but to save it. Unless you're an alien from another planet, you can be certain Jesus atoned for your sins and you are forgiven. You have peace with God. Thirdly, God joins us to Jesus in baptism. (Rom. 6) There we are joined with God's Name. He calls us from all others through the water and the Word to be his children. Fourthly, he calls us together with the rest of the body of his son to hear his word and receives the sacrament, the body and blood of the Lord Jesus, to seal us in our salvation.

So if you want to make certain you are God's elect be where God's elect are receiving what God's elect receive. It's that simple.

Lord Jesus Christ, we thank you for choosing us and preserving us with you word and sacrament and also for cutting the time short that we might not ever fall away from you. Keep us always together with your body that we may know we belong to you. Amen.

Lent Day 27 Friday
Read Gen 47:1–31

Gen 47:3-7 Pharaoh said to his brothers, "What is your occupation?" And they said to Pharaoh, "Your servants are shepherds, as our fathers were." (4) They said to Pharaoh, "We have come to sojourn in the land, for there is no pasture for your servants' flocks, for the famine is severe in the land of Canaan. And now, please let your servants dwell in the land of Goshen." (5) Then Pharaoh said to Joseph, "Your father and your brothers have come to you. (6) The land of Egypt is before you. Settle your father and your brothers in the best of the land. Let them settle in the land of Goshen, and if you know any able men among them, put them in charge of my livestock." (7) Then Joseph brought in Jacob his father and stood him before Pharaoh, and Jacob blessed Pharaoh.

The Lord had blessed Jacob in his family through the disaster of the relationships between his sons. He had taken the murderous and hateful thoughts of Joseph's brothers and turned into life for them and their families. The Lord had bless Joseph that he would find favor in Pharaoh's eyes and become head of Egypt and to provide a plan for saving both Israel and Egypt. Now we see the culmination of that blessing. Pharaoh would give to Joseph and his family the good fertile land of Goshen. It was in the Nile delta which received the rich silt of the Nile and fertilized the land. There was good pasture there.

We then should not be surprised at what Jacob does. Jacob blesses Pharaoh. That is a function of the Church on earth. The Church is to be a blessing to the kings of the earth it lives under even if and maybe particularly when the kings of the earth persecute it.

Peter reminds us we are to blessing people, 1Pe 3:9 "Do not repay evil for evil or reviling for reviling, but on the contrary, bless, for to this you were called, that you may obtain a blessing." And James in chapter 3 also reminds us of this vocation. Of course Jesus tells us this, Luk 6:28 "bless those who curse you, pray for those who abuse you." And so does St. Paul, Rom 12:14 "Bless those who persecute you; bless and do not curse them."

Specifically St. Paul reminds us to pray for those in authority, 1Ti 2:1-4 "First of all, then, I urge that supplications, prayers, intercessions, and thanksgivings be made for all people, (2) for kings and all who are in high positions, that we may lead a peaceful and quiet life, godly and dignified in every way. (3) This is good, and it is pleasing in the sight of God our Savior, (4) who desires all people to be saved and to come to the knowledge of the truth." St. Paul gives two good reasons for this. One is for the Church that it might live in peace and two that they might come to a saving knowledge of the truth.

Lord, God heavenly Father, you have ordained powers and authorities in the world. We pray you would bless them with wisdom so they may lead their people with justice, mercy, truth and equity. We pray for their conversion to faith in Christ Jesus that they too may understand, believe and confess Jesus as their Lord now freely rather than when He returns and are forced to their condemnation. In Jesus' name we pray, Amen.

Lent Day 27 Friday
Read Mark 13:24–37
Mar 13:32-37 "But concerning that day or that hour, no one knows, not even the angels in heaven, nor the Son, but only the Father. (33) Be on guard, keep awake. For you do not know when the time will come. (34) It is like a man going on a journey, when he leaves home and puts his servants in charge, each with his work, and commands the doorkeeper to stay awake. (35) Therefore stay awake--for you do not know when the master of the house will come, in the evening, or at midnight, or when the rooster crows, or in the morning-- (36) lest he come suddenly and find you asleep. (37) And what I say to you I say to all: Stay awake."

Concerning the destruction of Jerusalem for the idolatry of the Jews, that has already taken place. Now we wait for the time for our Lord to return as he departed with the clouds. But he will return gloriously with all his angels and all the world will see him. It will not be a secret coming. But the secret as to when that coming will take place is not made known to us. We must wait for it faithfully with patience.

Since we do not know the time Jesus reminds to be on guard and keep awake. Obviously he doesn't indeed for us to never sleep. But we are not to be to living and believing as if he is not returning. To be awake is to be faithful to the confession of his name. We are to continually be studying his word, confessing his word and receiving it with preaching and the sacraments with other believers.

To be asleep is to be unfaithful. It is to not believe Jesus' word of promise and warning. The devil loves to lull Christians to sleep, to make them believe what they believe doesn't and what they do doesn't matter. Don't you believe him, he is a liar.

Be awake! Pay attention to what you believe, what you read, what you listen to because it will affect your faith. Pay attention to what you think, say and do. These things can affect not only you but the people around you.

We have his assurance as we continue in his word he will preserve us until the when he sends his angels to gather us from the four corners of the earth.

Lord Jesus Christ, grant us your Holy Spirit and faith that we may remain awake and not be found sleeping on the day of your return. Amen.

Lent Day 28 Saturday

Read Gen 49:29—50:7, 14–26

Gen 50:17 'Say to Joseph, "Please forgive the transgression of your brothers and their sin, because they did evil to you."' And now, please forgive the transgression of the servants of the God of your father." Joseph wept when they spoke to him…19 But Joseph said to them, "Do not fear, for am I in the place of God? (20) As for you, you meant evil against me, but God meant it for good, to bring it about that many people should be kept alive, as they are today. (21) So do not fear; I will provide for you and your little ones." Thus he comforted them and spoke kindly to them.

Now we see Joseph's brothers still didn't trust Joseph. They must of have thought Joseph was just waiting for their father to die, and then he was going to take care of them, i.e. put them to death. They didn't trust the mercy he had shown them when they first came to Egypt. Of course he did give them a rough time of it to prove themselves that they had changed. Joseph was living rent free in their heads and he didn't even want to. This is what life is like when we don't go and make amends to the people we have harmed.

But Joseph had learned of the mercy of God during his life. He was moved by their fear and he wept because he thought after their final meeting when they brought his dad and brother they could get back to living. He knew and trusted in the promises of the Lord. The Lord had promised Abraham, Isaac and Jacob they would become a great nation, that would include his brothers.

Judgment belongs to God is Joseph's belief and attitude. While certainly his brothers meant evil for Joseph, God had a plan and turned it around for good. No doubt St. Paul is thinking about this in Romans 8, "God works all things for good for those who love him, who have been called according to his purpose." Therefore based on this, Joseph is going to continue to protect his brothers and their families.

We should have the same attitude and beliefs as Joseph. We like Joseph, who have been called to Abraham's children through baptism should believe that we have been called by God and this promise belongs to us in all trials and tribulations. Like Joseph we should forgive those who sin against us as God in Christ Jesus forgives us. Unlike Joseph's brothers we should follow Jesus' command to make up with our accusers along the way and not let the sun go down with someone angry at us so we need not walk in fear all our days.

Heavenly Father, ever give us faith to trust in your divine providence over us as your children and grant us your Holy Spirit that we may forgive those who sin against us even as you have forgiven all who have sinned against you. In Jesus' name we pray. Amen.

Lent Day 28 Saturday

Read Mark 14:1–11

Mar 14:3-9 And while he was at Bethany in the house of Simon the leper, as he was reclining at table, a woman came with an alabaster flask of ointment of pure nard, very costly, and she broke the flask and poured it over his head… (6) But Jesus said, "Leave her alone. Why do you trouble her? She has done a beautiful thing to me. (7) For you always have the poor with you, and whenever you want, you can do good for them. But you will not always have me. (8) She has done what she could; she has anointed my body beforehand for burial. (9) And truly, I say to you, wherever the gospel is proclaimed in the whole world, what she has done will be told in memory of her."

Well verse is certainly fulfilled today. This woman pours very expensive perfume on Jesus' head anointing him. God had appointed her for this purpose to proclaim the good news. What good news? Jesus says, "She has anointed my body beforehand for burial." If Jesus is going to be buried then Jesus is going to die. When we celebrate the Lord's Supper we proclaim his death until he comes. But the disciples at the time simply didn't get it.

Now if Jesus dies it is because the sin of the world has been laid on him. He is anointed to be our great high priest who does not offer the blood of bulls and goats on the temple altar. He offers his very own blood as the atoning sacrifice for the sin of the world. Jesus, the high priest according to the order of Melchizedeck makes a propitiation for us by his death on the cross. Our sin is truly on Jesus and buried in the tomb. It is for this that this woman anoints Jesus.

Now the disciples scolded her for this. There are many times people in Church do what they can and are scolded for it. It's a wonder we have anyone in Church at all sometimes. But God's plans, Jesus' plans are often greater than our plans. We get caught up in what we think our program should be and Jesus is showing us a different plan through his children. Are our plans God's plans or are they own plans? We should ask ourselves this sometimes.

Jesus had been telling the disciples God's plans for chapters now. They just didn't get it. The messiah must suffer, die and on the third day rise again. It is just what Jesus did. Because of this you now have peace with God. The Father no longer holds your sins against you. He has separated them as far as east from the west. God's plans are a plan of providing forgiveness and reconciliation with the world. Everything else is secondary. Not unimportant, but secondary.

Lord Jesus Christ, help us always to see your primary purpose is to give us mercy. Help us to see you desire mercy more than sacrifice and help us to be merciful to those around us and then to sacrifice. Amen.

5th Sunday in Lent

Read Ex 1:1–22

Exo 1:15-17 Then the king of Egypt said to the Hebrew midwives, one of whom was named Shiphrah and the other Puah, (16) "When you serve as midwife to the Hebrew women and see them on the birthstool, if it is a son, you shall kill him, but if it is a daughter, she shall live." (17) But the midwives feared God and did not do as the king of Egypt commanded them, but let the male children live.

God is fulfilling the promise he made to Abraham, Isaac and Jacob. For four hundred years the children of Israel have been multiplying in Egypt. It is thought that a new dynasty had come to power just before the time of Moses that was not friendly to Semitic peoples. So since the Israelites were seen as displaced foreigners and were getting so numerous they posed a physical threat, the Pharaoh decided he needed to do something about it. He was going to kill off the boys, assimilate the girls and put the people under the whip to keep them under control.

The Israelite women though feared the Lord more than Pharaoh. Some may take exception of them lying but this may instruct us that love is fulfillment of the law and that we must obey God rather than men. We saw similar actions during World War II in places the Nazis were in control.

Through these actions of faith, the women preserved the Israelite people, allowed for Moses to be brought into the world, the instrument through whom the Lord was going to free his people, and the line of Jesus would be preserved.

As Joseph reminded us, the Pharaoh meant it for evil but meant it for good. Through the evil of the Pharaoh the Lord was going to show his glory to the Egyptians and to his people. We may be experiencing as manner of evil, trial, tribulations in our lives. People and the world that brings these things upon us mean it for evil. But God uses it for his good and for our good. We may not always see it. The Israelites rarely realized it or remembered it. But as we read the Scriptures we can see it is true.

The actions of the midwives should encourage us in our daily living in the Lord. There is so much stuff out there which may cause us to doubt God's mercy and love. There are lots of situations which may tempt us to not be faithful to God: few for those who read this are threatened with death for being faithful. But the courage and faithfulness of the midwives should encourage us to be faithful no matter what also.

On top of that, the Lord himself became of us, was tempted in every way like us, was threatened with death and did indeed suffer death for our sakes, so we may live before God eternally. In and with his strength we too may remain faithful, even unto death should the situation require it.

Heavenly Father, you helped the midwives remain faithful to you and you demonstrated your faithfulness to us in your son Jesus. Grant us your Spirit and faith that we too may be faithful like them to your Word and Promises.

5th Sunday in Lent
Read Mark 14:12–31

Mark 14:22-24 And as they were eating, he took bread, and after blessing it broke it and gave it to them, and said, "Take; this is my body." (23) And he took a cup, and when he had given thanks he gave it to them, and they all drank of it. (24) And he said to them, "This is my blood of the covenant, which is poured out for many.

One of the holiest mysteries of the Christian faith, how can this bread and wine be Christ body and blood and what does this mean? Jesus' word is a word of covenant. A covenant is a legal document and should be read literally. The words of a covenant mean what the words say. This is not a parable, a story or a vision. It is the covenant the Lord had promised long ago through the prophet Jeremiah, Jeremiah 31:33-34 But this is the covenant that I will make with the house of Israel after those days, declares the LORD: I will put my law within them, and I will write it on their hearts. And I will be their God, and they shall be my people. (34) And no longer shall each one teach his neighbor and each his brother, saying, 'Know the LORD,' for they shall all know me, from the least of them to the greatest, declares the LORD. For I will forgive their iniquity, and I will remember their sin no more."

This being the case, we must remember that it is the Creator and Sustainer of Heaven and Earth who is in the flesh making this covenant. If our Creator and God can take on human flesh and become one of us in every way excepting sin, he can certainly have the bread and wine become his very body and blood. His body and blood give us what he says it does the forgiveness of sins. In many places the New Testament talks about the forgiveness of sins through the blood of Christ. The Lord's Supper is one place that blood is applied to us. It is the covenant promised in Jeremiah. Here as we take the very body and blood of Christ in our hands and upon our lips we can be sure and certain that God forgives us our sins and remembers them no more. We can be certain that He has chosen us to people His people and He has given Himself to be our God. Here in the Lord's Supper we know the Lord i.e. He is a God who is gracious, kind, loving, merciful, patient and forgiving toward us. Here in the Lord's Supper He places His Law upon our hearts with the Holy Spirit and gives us a will, mind, and desire to keep and do it.

We are justified when we receive his blood in faith. (Rom. 5:9) We participate in his blood. (1 Cor. 10:16) We have redemption and are brought near to God through his blood. (Eph. 1:7, 2:13) His blood purifies our conscience. (Heb. 9:14) We receive forgiveness of sins. (1 John 1:7) Our robes are made white, i.e. our whole being is purified by the blood of Christ. (Rev. 7:14) When we receive Christ's body and blood in his sacrament, his covenant, we can be sure and certain that all these promises of God in Christ's blood are applied to us.

Heavenly Father, grant that we may partake of Christ's very body and blood in faith, that our faith may be strengthened, that our knowledge of you may be increased and that your Law may be placed upon our hearts what we may both desire and do your will on earth. In Jesus' name. Amen.

Lent Day 29 Monday
Read Ex 2:1–22
Exo 2:5-10 (5) Now the daughter of Pharaoh came down to bathe at the river, while her young women walked beside the river. She saw the basket among the reeds and sent her servant woman, and she took it. (6) When she opened it, she saw the child, and behold, the baby was crying. She took pity on him and said, "This is one of the Hebrews' children." (7) Then his sister said to Pharaoh's daughter, "Shall I go and call you a nurse from the Hebrew women to nurse the child for you?" (8) And Pharaoh's daughter said to her, "Go." So the girl went and called the child's mother. (9) And Pharaoh's daughter said to her, "Take this child away and nurse him for me, and I will give you your wages." So the woman took the child and nursed him. (10) When the child grew up, she brought him to Pharaoh's daughter, and he became her son. She named him Moses, "Because," she said, "I drew him out of the water."

Is the Lord a master manipulator of people and events or what? 400 years have passed since we left the children of Israel in Egypt. Things have changed just as God told Abraham they would. Egypt is no longer a friend to the Israelites. While they don't want to lose the resource the Egyptians want to keep them under control. God has other plans. He's going to take this one Israelite boy from the tribe of Levi and have him grow up in Pharaoh's house. Now just to clear up some misconception about Moses from every movie ever made, as we can see from the text here, everyone including Moses himself knew he was a Hebrew.

Now Moses would be prepared for his future purposes of the Lord in Pharaoh's house. He'd get the best education, military training, and leadership training in the country. God was preparing him for something great. He was going to lead the Israelite nation out of Egypt and lead them in the wilderness for 40+ years and have them battle inhabitants along the way. He would have to organize them and move them. He would have to be better at logistics than UPS.

Jesus would fulfill Moses. Having similar humble beginnings he would escape the flood coming out of the dragon's mouth in the form of Herod's soldiers who sought his life as a child. Jesus also would come out of Egypt. As to Jesus' training we can only assume it was typical for his station in life. But God had a plan for Jesus and he manipulated the times and the people to have Jesus crucified for the sin of the world so all men may receive eternal life through his sacrifice. The account of Moses isn't about God has a great plan for your life in mundane things. He may intend for you to be a day laborer, a simple mother, or other such vocations the world does not think much about. But God's ultimate plan for you in Christ Jesus is to enter eternal life with him as his child. And that isn't anything to sneeze at.

Lord God, Heavenly Father, you may not have some grand design for my life in this age but I thank you for the grand purpose you have for me in the world to come. In Jesus' name, Amen.

Lent Day 29 Monday
Read Mark 14:32–52
Mar 14:35-36 And going a little farther, he fell on the ground and prayed that, if it were possible, the hour might pass from him. (36) And he said, "Abba, Father, all things are possible for you. Remove this cup from me. Yet not what I will, but what you will."

So horrible was the suffering Jesus was going to undergo he ask his Father in heaven to not let him to suffer it. If we were just looking at what happens when you're crucified it is certainly understandable. The beatings, the insults, exposure to the sun, the nailing and a long drawn out suffocation are enough for me to want to opt out. But Jesus is doing more than that and he knows it. He will become sin. Becoming sin would in our minds (sinful as they are) be equivalent of an innocent being raped. Jesus is defiled on the cross.

Not only is Jesus defiled on the cross, he is also punished for the sins of us all. The curse of God rest on him though he obeyed the law of God perfectly. Jesus knows he will be rejected by the Father. His blood must be spilt for the Father to be reconciled to the World.

Yet Jesus is not defiant as the first Adam was. He submits himself to the will of the Father. "Not what I will, but what you will" Jesus prays. If there was another way to accomplish the salvation of the world that didn't involve the crucifixion Jesus wanted to do it. But it the Father says this is the way it has to be, Jesus is good with it. For our Lord Jesus Christ always aligns his will with the Father's, for Jesus not only has himself in mind but most importantly he has us in mind and wants what is best for us. "But for the joy set before him, he scorned the shame."

Now as we focus on Jesus as he goes to his cross we who follow him must do likewise. We will experience in our lives all sorts of pain and suffering. Sometimes physical, sometimes emotional and sometimes spiritual but we will suffer. Each of us must bear our own cross. But it's not that bad. We only have to bear our cross. Jesus on the cross bears the crosses of us all.

And now as we put our trust in him that he has borne our cross the cross we bear is no longer our own but Jesus'. But it's only the part that Jesus bore for us individually. Jesus' sufferings overflow into our life. But St. Paul promises in 1 Cor. 1 that as the sufferings of Christ's overflow into our life, so too does his comfort. So when we are suffering our cross let us not shake our fist at God. Instead let us join with Christ in the garden, not my will be done but yours.

Gracious God, Heavenly Father, as the sufferings of Christ overflow into our lives as we trust in him, help us to bear up patiently under them knowing our Lord Jesus has already borne these for us on his cross. Amen.

Lent Day 30 Tuesday
Read Ex 2:23—3:22
Exo 2:23-24 During those many days the king of Egypt died, and the people of Israel groaned because of their slavery and cried out for help. Their cry for rescue from slavery came up to God. (24) And God heard their groaning, and God remembered his covenant with Abraham, with Isaac, and with Jacob. Exo 3:6-9 And he said, "I am the God of your father, the God of Abraham, the God of Isaac, and the God of Jacob." And Moses hid his face, for he was afraid to look at God. (7) Then the LORD said, "I have surely seen the affliction of my people who are in Egypt and have heard their cry because of their taskmasters. I know their sufferings…"

God remembers. Well being omniscient and all one would expect God to be able to do that and to do that. God is remembering his people and the covenant he made with the patriarchs, Abraham, Isaac and Jacob.

What was this covenant? That the Lord would bless Abraham so he would have descendents like the stars in the sky and the dusk of the earth. The Israelites were now in the 3 million plus category. Promise fulfilled! Now he is going to deliver the land of the Canaanites into their hands. It will take a couple of centuries for them to wipe out the inhabitants of the land due to their sins but that part of the covenant will be fulfilled by the time of Solomon.

God takes his time in fulfilling what he promised. Some things just take time in human events. It would be another couple of millennia before the Lord, the God of Abraham, Isaac and Jacob before the third part of the covenant would be fulfilled. That would be the seed (singular) of Abraham would be a blessing to all nations. That is fulfilled in Jesus of Nazareth. In Jesus all nations of the world are blessed because in him all nations are reconciled to God through his blood.

It is in Jesus of Nazareth a new covenant is established one that would supersede the Mosaic covenant. This is the new covenant that the Lord Jesus Christ, our God remembers now: "I will forgive them their sins and remember them no more. I will be their God and they will be my people." Jesus instituted this on the night he was betrayed. We call it the Lord's Supper. When we celebrate it God remembers and we remember this new covenant and rejoice in it.

Lord God, heavenly Father we do than you that you are a God who remembers and performs the terms of the covenant. Help us to remember and believe all you have done for us in Christ Jesus. In Jesus' name we pray, Amen.

Lent Day 30 Tuesday
Read Mark 14:53–72
Mar 14:60-64 And the high priest stood up in the midst and asked Jesus, "Have you no answer to make? What is it that these men testify against you?" (61) But he remained silent and made no answer. Again the high priest asked him, "Are you the Christ, the Son of the Blessed?" (62) And Jesus said, "I am, and you will see the Son of Man seated at the right hand of Power, and coming with the clouds of heaven."

In the midst of the silliness that the History Channel, Discovery, TLC, the news and the magazines usually put out this year from so called scholars about how Jesus was misunderstood, if the above account is correct, and I believe it is, then neither Jesus nor the court misunderstood Jesus.

They understood the Christ was to be the Son of God who is the Son of Man described by Daniel. That means they understood the Christ, David's descended would also be divine. Jesus tells them he is that one they are expecting. If they didn't understand the Messiah to be a divine descendent of David then they would not be asking the question. And because Jesus answers in the affirmative and they don't believe him, he is blaspheming. Jesus can only be blaspheming if he isn't who he says he is and who they expect the messiah to be. If they understood the messiah to be only human, the high priest question and Jesus' reply could not get Jesus condemned for blasphemy.

So what are we to do with this? Jesus is truly man, a descendent of David. Jesus is son of the Most High God, he is God. Now the God-Man goes to the cross and dies. How can this be? How can God die? He is not only God but also Man. So the Son of Man, the Son of the Blessed, dies on the cross according to his human nature. But the person, Jesus, the Son of Man, i.e. the Son of God, experiences it. It is similar to the fact that your spirit does not experience death, yet never the less, because you are your body also, you do experience death. Of course if you are not a Christian, you will experience death according to both natures (human and spirit/soul) [that does not mean your spirit/soul is annihilated, just that it doesn't have the life of God, it still is conscience).

If this is true than not only it your soul atoned for but your body as well. Humans are meant to be embodied spirits. So Jesus redeems the whole person through his death on the cross. That means he has redeemed in particular, you—your body and soul and person.

Lord help us ever to keep the incarnation ever before our eyes even in your death that we may know our redemption. Amen.

Lent Day 31 Wednesday
Read Ex 4:1–18
Exo 4:11-15 Then the LORD said to him, "Who has made man's mouth? Who makes him mute, or deaf, or seeing, or blind? Is it not I, the LORD? (12) now therefore go, and I will be with your mouth and teach you what you shall speak." (13) But he said, "Oh, my Lord, please send someone else." (14) Then the anger of the LORD was kindled against Moses and he said, "Is there not Aaron, your brother, the Levite? I know that he can speak well. Behold, he is coming out to meet you, and when he sees you, he will be glad in his heart. (15) You shall speak to him and put the words in his mouth, and I will be with your mouth and with his mouth and will teach you both what to do.

In American society we don't think much of the pastoral office. While few ever would put their hand to the plow they think any old Tom, Dick and Harry can do it. Perhaps they are right to a certain extent. God can and does all sorts of men to be brought into the office of the Holy Ministry. But my point this day is not so much the man whom God has called to be a pastor but who does he represent and who does he speak for? Indeed, who is speaking in and through him?

In today's lesson we see God choosing Moses to be his mouthpiece and instrument to deliver the Israelites. He doesn't want to do it. Few men called into the ministry do. But we're face up against God who gives us the word he gives to Moses, "Who has made man's mouth? Who makes him mute, or deaf, or seeing, or blind? Is it not I, the LORD?" Scientist often wonder what is the cause of man's speech. Well it is God. God gives all of us the gift of speech. But now the Lord gives a special Word which will encourage Moses and Aaron, "Now therefore go, and I will be with your mouth and teach you what you shall speak."

Today's ministers have the same promise from Jesus. "Mar 13:11 And when they bring you to trial and deliver you over, do not be anxious beforehand what you are to say, but say whatever is given you in that hour, for it is not you who speak, but the Holy Spirit." When the minister of God speaks he speaks the very words of God. Or at least he should. Prophets have control over what they say even if it is inspired by the Holy Spirit, 1Co 14:32 "and the spirits of prophets are subject to prophets." We preach the Word of God. 1Th 2:13 "And we also thank God constantly for this, that when you received the word of God, which you heard from us, you accepted it not as the word of men but as what it really is, the word of God, which is at work in you believers."

Unless you can prove the minister's Word is not the Word of God then you should accept it as such and believe, trust and obey it as such. They speak as those who are accountable for your souls. God puts into their mouths what to say if only for the sake of the office which He created.

O Holy Spirit, put the Word of God on the mouths of your pastors that they may feed us with the very Word of God, Jesus Christ our Lord so we may be edified they themselves gloried and rewarded for their work when Jesus returns for all those who put their trust in His Word. In Jesus' name we pray, Amen.

Lent Day 31 Wednesday

Read Mark 15:1–15

Mar 15:9-14 And he answered them, saying, "Do you want me to release for you the King of the Jews?" . . . (12) And Pilate again said to them, "Then what shall I do with the man you call the King of the Jews?" (13) And they cried out again, "Crucify him." (14) And Pilate said to them, "Why, what evil has he done?" But they shouted all the more, "Crucify him."

It is interesting that in Matthew and Mark Pilate says to the Jews shall I crucify the one "you" call king or messiah. It is only at the cross they object to his charges to say "Say he claimed to be king." In John, they do reject the claim outright, but even more so, they say we have no king but Caesar. The Lord is the king of the Jews in the Old Testament.

But that is who Jesus is. Jesus is the king of the Jews. Not only is he king through the Davidic line, but Jesus is the king of the Jews before Saul. For Jesus is the Lord. So caught up were the Jews they crucified their true and always king. As Peter would later preach, "You crucified the Lord of Glory; you killed the author of life."

After the resurrection, many repented and believed on their king who is the Lord. Many did not and still do not. And we must pray for their conversion to trust the one who brought them out of Egypt, Jesus the Messiah.

But crucified is what Jesus must be. If he is not killed then we will continue in sin and death. The sin of the world must be placed on him. He must become our scapegoat. Indeed Jesus fulfills it.

Therefore our sins have been carried away. His blood has made atonement for them. Because of his sacrifice we can trust him and call him king, king of the universe.

Lord ever help us to believe you are our king. Grant repentance to your fallen people who still reject that we all together with one voice cry out Hosanna! Amen.

Lent Day 32 Thursday
Read Ex 4:19–31
Exo 4:28-31 And Moses told Aaron all the words of the LORD with which he had sent him to speak, and all the signs that he had commanded him to do… (30) Aaron spoke all the words that the LORD had spoken to Moses and did the signs in the sight of the people. (31) And the people believed; and when they heard that the LORD had visited the people of Israel and that he had seen their affliction, they bowed their heads and worshiped.

The Faith of the Lord is transmitted by the Word of the Lord. Moses tells Aaron all that the Lord had spoken to him and all the signs he was commanded to do and Aaron believed him. As far as we know, Aaron saw none of the signs. He only knew what Moses had told him. When they gather all the elders of Israel, Aaron, the mouthpiece of Moses, speaks all that Moses has told him and then and did the signs in the sight of the people. Now these signs are not the great works of God to follow but rather some tokens by which the people may recognize Moses and Aaron are true prophets.

Now the people believed. They had heard that the Lord had visited them in their distress. He had seen their affliction and was going to deliver them from it. In faith they bow down and worshipped the Lord.

Now the Lord has visited us. He visited us in the person of Jesus. Jesus did not come to save us from Pharaoh but from sin, death and the power of the devil. Jesus preached the Word of God among and worked many signs. The apostles as the elders of Israel received that Word and preached it with power and signs to confirm that Word. People believed that God had visited us and they passed that Word on to us to this day.

He has given us tokens also with the word, baptism and the Lord's Supper. These signs give us what they say they are: life and salvation. Through the word we too believe and have our faith confirmed by these tokens of faith. But when was the last time you bowed down? Is your faith followed by worshipping the Lord? If we believe what God has done for us in Christ Jesus then it should be followed by serving the Lord, individually and collectively.

Heavenly Father, you sent your son Jesus Christ that he might do your works and give us your word so we may believe in him and be delivered from sin, death and the devil. Give us faith that we may receive this and worship you as you desired to be served. In Jesus' name we pray, Amen.

Lent Day 32 Thursday
Read Mark 15:16–32
Mar 15:26-27 And the inscription of the charge against him read, "The King of the Jews." (27) And with him they crucified two robbers, one on his right and one on his left.

Earlier in Mark two of the apostles' asked Jesus, "Grant us to sit, one at your right hand and one at your left, in your glory." Mar 10:37   And Jesus answered, "but to sit at my right hand or at my left is not mine to grant, but it is for those for whom it has been prepared." Mar 10:40 Now we see for who it is prepared for Jesus enters his glory on the cross. There despite the witness of unbelieving Pilate Jesus is recognized as the King of the Jews. On the cross God is crucified. Paul tells us, "They crucified the Lord of glory."

This was to fulfill the prophecy, "Therefore I will divide him a portion with the many, and he shall divide the spoil with the strong, because he poured out his soul to death and was numbered with the transgressors; yet he bore the sin of many, and makes intercession for the transgressors." (Isa 53:12) Being numbered with transgressors as he enters his glory he has two transgressors one on his left and one on his right. Both of them rail against Jesus and insult him. Something happens along the way though and one of them repents.

The King of the Jews lifted up for all to see. Jesus is the king of the Jews. The king of the Jews is God Almighty, the Lord, the God of Abraham, Isaac and Jacob is crucified. It is beyond imagination. How can God die? How can God become man? Why does he allow this to happen to himself? " . . . Jesus the founder and perfecter of our faith, who for the joy that was set before him endured the cross, despising the shame, and is seated at the right hand of the throne of God. (Heb 12:2) The joy set before him puts him on the cross and keeps him on the cross. God loves us. That's why he does it. "In this is love, not that we have loved God but that he loved us and sent his Son to be the propitiation for our sins."(1Jn 4:10) And the hows? Nothing is impossible with God.

O King of the universe, we thank you for being crucified for us and for all mankind. Grant us faith to believe it and courage to share this good news with all come across our path that we might rightly attribute all glory to your name Jesus. Amen.

Lent Day 33 Friday
Read Ex 5:1—6:1
Exo 5:22-6:1 Then Moses turned to the LORD and said, "O Lord, why have you done evil to this people? Why did you ever send me? (23) For since I came to Pharaoh to speak in your name, he has done evil to this people, and you have not delivered your people at all." (6:1) But the LORD said to Moses, "Now you shall see what I will do to Pharaoh; for with a strong hand he will send them out, and with a strong hand he will drive them out of his land."

Well it seemed like a reasonable request, "Let us go and worship our God in the wilderness for several days." But God had a plan. Pharaoh already was hardened against the Israelites but now he had it set in his mind they had too much time on their hands. The Lord therefore hardened his heart even more and set it against the Israelites. They had to gather their own straw for the bricks and the Israelites in charge of their brethren were beaten if they did not still come up with the same quota, which they didn't. They were then set against Moses and Aaron.

Moses, in turn, turns to the Lord. "Lord, why did you do this? Why did you send me? Nothing has happened but evil since I got here." How often do we too wonder what the Lord is doing when we think we are doing everything correctly? Indeed, we might be doing everything, as humanly possible what the Lord has given us to do. Yet everything seems to be going wrong. I know pastors often feel this way. But the rest of God's people also have this happen to them as well. It seems as if God is against us. This is the mystery of bearing the cross. The Lord is not against us. He just has bigger plans than we can comprehend at the moment. Our faith is being purified.

Now the Lord answers Moses (we wish we could hear the voice of the Lord who would explain things to us) and tells him now you will see what I will do to Pharaoh and how with a powerful hand he will not only set them free but drive them out. As we shall see in upcoming days, it won't be as quick as we might have hoped. Moses and the Israelites were wondering, "When are you going to get this done?" It had been 400 years since they've been in Egypt. The majority of the suffering was only for the last several generations of Israelites from what I can tell. But God's timing is not our timing.

I believe it is a fact; we don't always see what the Lord Jesus is doing in our lives or see the end of it while we are still breathing. The sufferings we endure may be for our lifetime and it is only when we see the face of God that we will finally understand what he was up to that whole time. This requires faith. We have God's promises in Christ Jesus. Through these promise we become partakers of the divine nature (2 Peter 1:4). The Israelites had the Lord's promises and believed, but they faltered too sometimes.

Heavenly Father, grant us faith to believe you know what you are doing and that what we endure in this life is for our good and your glory so we may see your face and be participants in your divine glory. In Jesus' name we pray. Amen.

Lent Day 33 Friday
Read Mark 15:33–47
And at the ninth hour Jesus cried with a loud voice, "Eloi, Eloi, lema sabachthani?" which means, "My God, my God, why have you forsaken me?"
(Mar 15:34)

Well if you really want to know what's going on go read Psalm 22. Finished? Good. But let's get to the real scandal here: Jesus the only begotten Son of God from all eternity. True God and True Man, perfect man, totally obedient to the Father in heave is forsaken by God. This can't be you say. How can God the Father forsake his Son? If Jesus isn't truly forsaken then you are still in your sins. Jesus died for nothing. In fact, if Jesus isn't forsaken then Jesus doesn't die. Jesus is forsaken by God for your sake, on your behalf so you are accepted by the Father.

Why is Jesus forsaken? For our sake he made him to be sin who knew no sin, so that in him we might become the righteousness of God. (2Co 5:21) Christ redeemed us from the curse of the law by becoming a curse for us--for it is written, "Cursed is everyone who is hanged on a tree"-- (Gal 3:13) So if Jesus isn't forsaken then he did not become sin. If Jesus isn't forsaken then he isn't cursed. And if that were true, you wouldn't become the righteousness of God or redeemed from the curse of the law.

The good news is Jesus is forsaken so you might become the righteousness of God and be redeemed from the curse of the law. It's not as if though Jesus really has to ask the question. It is asked for your sake. So you may believe what was written in Ps. 22. You did go read Psalm 22?

He has not despised or abhorred the affliction of the afflicted, and he has not hidden his face from him, but has heard, when he cried to him. From you comes my praise in the great congregation; my vows I will perform before those who fear him. The afflicted shall eat and be satisfied; those who seek him shall praise the LORD! May your hearts live forever! All the ends of the earth shall remember and turn to the LORD, and all the families of the nations shall worship before you.
(Psa 22:24-27)

Lord Jesus Christ we thank you for being forsaken for us that we might be acceptable to God the Father. Grant such faith always to believe you have done this for us. Amen.

Lent Day 34 Saturday
Read Ex 7:1–25
Exo 7:1-6 And the LORD said to Moses, "See, I have made you like God to Pharaoh, and your brother Aaron shall be your prophet. (2) You shall speak all that I command you, and your brother Aaron shall tell Pharaoh to let the people of Israel go out of his land. (3) But I will harden Pharaoh's heart, and though I multiply my signs and wonders in the land of Egypt,…"

Now this is one of main themes of the early part of Exodus if not the whole the whole scriptures. What is that you say? That mankind comes to know the Lord. Here in particular is that Pharaoh and the Egyptians come to the know the Lord. Unfortunately for them they are going to get to know the Lord from his judgment side. They are going to learn about his power and might. The Lord still calls out to the world from his judgment side with disasters, calamities and the like calling us to repentance.

On the other hand the Israelites, God's chosen people are going to get the knowledge the Lord in a whole different sense, the sense the Lord really wants to be known. They will know the Lord as a great deliverer. He will free them from the land of bondage and of misery. They will be shown him who is merciful, kind, patience and bound to a covenantal love he had placed himself.

In the New Testament this is also a theme. Jeremiah says, Jer 31:34 "And no longer shall each one teach his neighbor and each his brother, saying, 'Know the LORD,' for they shall all know me, from the least of them to the greatest, declares the LORD. For I will forgive their iniquity, and I will remember their sin no more." Jesus says to the Jews, John 8:19 "You know neither me nor my Father. If you knew me, you would know my Father also." To his disciples he says, John 14:9 "Whoever has seen me has seen the Father. How can you say, 'Show us the Father'? Concerning those who would come after the apostles he says, "John 10:27 My sheep hear my voice, and I know them, and they follow me." And St. Paul testifies, 1Co 13:12 "For now we see in a mirror dimly, but then face to face. Now I know in part; then I shall know fully, even as I have been fully known."

God does not want to be a hidden quality. But to know the Lord as he wants to be known, one can only know him in Jesus Christ. Jesus Christ makes his Father known as the one who his patient, kind, long-suffering, forgiving and love. But apart from Christ Jesus you simply will not know the Lord this way. But you know him and will know him as one who brings judgment. How do you want to know him?

Lord Jesus Christ, you reveal to us the Father in the manner in which he wants to be know through faith your work in you innocent suffering, death and resurrection. Grant us faith to know you that we may know the Father as well. Amen.

Lent Day 34 Saturday

Read Mark 16:1–20

And entering the tomb, they saw a young man sitting on the right side, dressed in a white robe, and they were alarmed. And he said to them, "Do not be alarmed. You seek Jesus of Nazareth, who was crucified. He has risen; he is not here. See the place where they laid him. (Mar 16:5-6)

At first glance one may wonder what on earth we are doing reading the resurrection a week before the Crucifixion and the Resurrection. Yet this is where the daily lectionary has led us. Why did they have us end up here?

I don't know for sure. But what is tomorrow? That's right! It's Palm Sunday. Palm Sunday is when we celebrate our Lord Jesus Christ entering Jerusalem as the King of the Jews. This indeed was his earthly entrance to his earthly title. But here in the resurrection we have something else. Now in the resurrection, Jesus has battled sin, death, and the power of the devil and has defeated them all. He has conquered the god of this world. He has conquered temptation to sin. He has conquered our enemy Death.

So now in his resurrection Jesus goes on to enter the heavenly Jerusalem to take up his rightful place, not just as King of the Jews or King of Israel, or even King of the World, but now he takes his place as King of the Universe. All that is seen and unseen, everything in all creation, in heaven and on earth, Jesus is Lord of all. Most importantly of all, Jesus is Lord of all for you.

Amazing thing the resurrection.

O Lord our God, Jesus of Nazareth, even as you have been declared Lord of all by your resurrection, grant us faith that we might willingly be your subjects and have you be Lord over us. Amen.

Palm Sunday

Read Ex 8:1–32

Exo 8: 2 But on that day I will set apart the land of Goshen, where my people dwell, so that no swarms of flies shall be there, that you may know that I am the LORD in the midst of the earth. (23) Thus I will put a division between my people and your people. Tomorrow this sign shall happen."""…31 And the LORD did as Moses asked, and removed the swarms of flies from Pharaoh, from his servants, and from his people; not one remained. (32) But Pharaoh hardened his heart this time also, and did not let the people go.

What kind of God smites people with frogs? Apparently the Egyptians didn't appreciate them. Stranger yet, the magicians also produced frogs (now they did it to show Moses wasn't anything special). But the Moses produced gnats the Egyptian magicians were stumped and they realized this was the finger of God. Now the reason the Lord put these plagues upon the land so was they would know that the Lord is in the midst of the earth. Like yesterday, they would know the Lord from judgment.

Now the Pharaoh every time says he repents. "If you just fix this thing for me Lord, I swear I'll never do it again!" We've said this prayer and many who have reaped the natural consequences of their sinful habits are prone to pray this prayer a lot. Like Pharaoh, the Lord listens but Pharaoh and we harden our hearts and we're back in the mire.

Now when the Lord sends the flies he doesn't something different here and it will continue for all the following plagues. The rest of the plagues do not fall upon the land of Israelites but only upon the Egyptians. The final plague falls upon everyone who did not have faith. This is also reflected in the plagues of Revelation. Some things happen to everyone and some things only come upon those who aren't baptized and have faith.

Now Pharaoh again did not repent though the opportunity was there. He again hardened his heart against the Lord and the Israelites. Now what are we going to do? Are we too going to harden our hearts after God delivers us from whatever trouble we have gotten ourselves into again? Or are we going to thank the Lord Jesus Christ for the mercy bestowed and live out the gift of grace he has given us? In the book of Revelation, after many of the plagues, the people still did not repent. What are you going to do?

Heavenly Father, ever give us your grace that we may repent of our sins, trust in Christ and continue to follow Jesus every day of our lives and do not let us harden our hearts but grant us lives of continual repentance. In Jesus' name we pray. Amen.

Palm Sunday
Read Heb 1:1–14

He is the radiance of the glory of God and the exact imprint of his nature, and he upholds the universe by the word of his power. After making purification for sins, he sat down at the right hand of the Majesty on high, (Heb 1:3) But of the Son he says, "Your throne, O God, is forever and ever, the scepter of uprightness is the scepter of your kingdom. (Heb 1:8)

This is one of those things that make the crucifixion mysterious when we really think about it. Just who was crucified? What was he who was crucified? No doubt thousands upon thousands of people were crucified but Jesus is different.

Who and what is Jesus? Jesus is the radiance of the glory of God. Jesus is the exact imprint of the Father's nature. Jesus upholds the universe by the power of his word. Jesus is God whose throne is forever and ever.

Peter tells us when he preaches to the Jews, "You have killed the author of life." St. Paul tells us, "They crucified the Lord of Glory." But Jesus is God. How can God die? If God can die but he could stop it why would he allow himself to be killed?

Jesus is God, the Son of God, and the Word of God having taken on human flesh, which is everything necessary to be truly human in every way. The person of the Son of God, in his human flesh experiences the sin of world being placed on him. He experiences the punishment for that sin in his flesh and in his soul. Jesus, the God Man, experiences death, damnation, and hell, for the world on the cross. His blood has made purification for the sin of the world as John the Baptist proclaims in John ch. 1.

But why would he do that? Jesus tells us in John 3, "For God so loved the world, that he gave his only Son, that whoever believes in him should not perish but have eternal life. (John 3:16) And again in 1 John In this is love, not that we have loved God but that he loved us and sent his Son to be the propitiation for our sins. (1Jn 4:10)

It is the love of God that impels Jesus Christ to die for the sin of the world. If Jesus dies for the sin of the world, then he dies for you because he loves you. What great love would sacrifice itself for those who've rebelled against him. But Jesus and the Father do love you and that's why Jesus became flesh and went to the cross.

We thank you my heavenly Father that you have sent your Son, Jesus, into the flesh to die for the sin of the world and therefore died for my sin. Ever grant me such faith to believe this and from there to love you and love my neighbor. Amen.

Lent Day 35 Monday
Read Ex 9:1–28
Exo 9:16 "But for this purpose I have raised you up, to show you my power, so that my name may be proclaimed in all the earth…19 Now therefore send, get your livestock and all that you have in the field into safe shelter, for every man and beast that is in the field and is not brought home will die when the hail falls on them."

Like the last couple of plagues the following plagues also fall only upon the land of Egypt. Goshen, where the Israelites lived, were not affected by the Lord's plagues. God makes a distinction between those who believe in him and those who do not. As said yesterday, this theme will be picked up again in the book of Revelation.

But now, with the plague of hail, the Lord offers a chance for the Egyptians to show they have faith in the word of the Lord. The Lord warns them he is bringing a great hail upon the land. Well those who have been watching and believe what the Lord can and will do take the precautions the Lord gives. They bring into shelter anything they don't want ruined by the hail. Those who don't believe the Lord's word leave their goods out in the open and they are destroyed by the hail.

Now in the two plagues before this, Pharaoh didn't repent and his heart was just hardened. This event was so disastrous it broke even his stony heart and he repented. He asked Moses for help and the Lord relented. But like so many of us, once we are out of trouble we're right back in the thick of things, Pharaoh hardened his heart. Now the Lord is using the hardness of Pharaoh's heart to have the name of Lord proclaimed in all the earth. It was the reason the Lord had raised him to this position. Though he may king of all Egypt and think he is a god, those in positions of authority upon the earth are there by God's doing. Therefore, we Christians should not fear the rulers of the world. Like Pharaoh, God has placed them there for his purposes, namely the spreading of the Gospel, the proclamation of the good news of Jesus Christ. While they serve to have order and peace in the world, the Lord raises some for his divine purpose of glorifying his name. Whether they do good or evil, they are his servants.

Heavenly Father, we pray for all those in positions of authority that they may be led by your good wisdom that we, your people, may live our lives in quietness and peace, to the glory of your holy name and the glory of Jesus Christ. In His name we pray. Amen.

Lent Day 35 Monday
Read Heb 2:1–18
Heb 2:1-3 Therefore we must pay much closer attention to what we have heard, lest we drift away from it… 10 For it was fitting that he, for whom and by whom all things exist, in bringing many sons to glory, should make the founder of their salvation perfect through suffering. (11) For he who sanctifies and those who are sanctified all have one source…14 Since therefore the children share in flesh and blood, he himself likewise partook of the same things, that through death he might destroy the one who has the power of death, that is, the devil, (15) and deliver all those who through fear of death were subject to lifelong slavery….

You see, God in the Scriptures is very concerned that we pay attention to what is taught, i.e. doctrine. For only correct doctrine can create faith and receive such a great salvation. A false faith does not receive salvation from Jesus Christ.

And what is this correct teaching or doctrine? The Creator and Sustainer of the universe suffered for our sake and is the foundation of our salvation. By and through Jesus' suffering the Father brings us to glory, the glory of the only unbegotten Son, Jesus Christ. Jesus' source is the Father from eternity. The Father through His Son Jesus is the source of our life, eternal life. Jesus has sanctified us by the water and the Word, baptism and faith in the promises of baptism. He sanctifies us through His Supper, His body and blood.

Jesus shared in our flesh and blood and underwent our trials, temptations and became a sin offering for us. Jesus shared in our death that he might destroy the one who has the power over death, that is the devil. Jesus rose from the dead, victorious over Hades, Sin and Satan. We need not fear death any longer. The fear of death no longer has to drive our lives and how we live for we know in Christ, we live forever. We who have faith in the Son, Jesus Christ, are slaves of Christ and Righteousness now. Our old taskmaster can no longer order us about, though he tries. He tries to make us think the old order of things is still in place. He tries to make us believe God cannot and will not forgive us our sins. He tries to make us fear death and have that cause to think, speak and commit sins and drive a wedge between us and our heavenly Father. But no, he is defeated.

Jesus now is our high priest before God. He intercedes for us and stands before the Father pleading mercy for us. Jesus is our propitiation for our sins. Jesus is the atoning blood upon the mercy seat of the Father. Jesus is our mercy from the Father. Being made like us in every way excepting sin and having under gone temptation like us, Jesus understands our weakness and his able to help us in them. Because he was tempted he can help us when tempted, believing he has overcome the tempter.

Lord Jesus Christ, ever plead to your Father in heaven to give us strength to not fall into temptation when it comes and if we do fall, plead your blood in the Father's ear that we may not be held accountable for them and show Him your propitious sacrifice. Amen.

Lent Day 36 Tuesday
Read Ex 9:29—10:20
Exodus 9:29-34 29 Moses said to him, "As soon as I have gone out of the city, I will stretch out my hands to the Lord. The thunder will cease, and there will be no more hail, so that you may know that the earth is the Lord's. 30 But as for you and your servants, I know that you do not yet fear the Lord God." …33 So Moses went out of the city from Pharaoh and stretched out his hands to the Lord, and the thunder and the hail ceased, and the rain no longer poured upon the earth. 34 But when Pharaoh saw that the rain and the hail and the thunder had ceased, he sinned yet again and hardened his heart, he and his servants.

Pharaoh is like your typical alcoholic at about 3 am and 10 am in the morning. Kneeling at the porcelain altar he cries out to whatever god he thinks he believes in or acknowledges and says, "I swear if you get me out of this, I'll never do it again." Yet we know by 1 pm at the latest if he is awake, he'll be sippin' a little bit of the hair of the dog that bit him and he'll be at that altar again soon. We note a couple things about this incident with Pharaoh. First, it is Pharaoh who hardens his heart against the Lord before the Lord begins to harden Pharaoh's heart. Second, that is the way it is with us.

You don't need to be an alcoholic to act this way, but it helps. Indeed, we are all addicted to sin. We can never get enough of it. We turn to it to solve all our problems in life. When it comes around and bites us in the rear, which it always does, we turn to the invisible deity and cry out, "If you get me out of this, I swear, I'll never do it again." And it seems to be more often than not the Lord goes, "Why not." And lo and behold we are out of whatever mess we made for ourselves. Then we forget the deity who has delivered us and we go back to doing whatever it was that got us through the night before we prayed.

God in Christ Jesus does want to and does indeed deliver us from sin, death and the power of the devil. He renews our minds and gives us the Holy Spirit, so we may turn from depending on sin and start depending on and trusting in Christ Jesus in our every need. He's even given us a prayer, the Lord's Prayer or Our Father that we can pray every day and whenever we feel we need assistance. We simply need to trust that God the Father hears and answers that prayer and live as if indeed the help has come. Jesus has taught us that when we pray give thanks as if you have already received it.

Lord Jesus Christ, by your suffering and death, by your resurrection, you have freed us from our addicted dependence upon sin to supply us our every need. Grant unto to us true repentance that we not harden our hearts and return to the sin that enslaves us. Amen.

Lent Day 36 Tuesday
Read Heb 3:1–19

Heb 3:5-6 Now Moses was faithful in all God's house as a servant, to testify to the things that were to be spoken later, (6) but Christ is faithful over God's house as a son. And we are his house if indeed we hold fast our confidence and our boasting in our hope… 14 For we have come to share in Christ, if indeed we hold our original confidence firm to the end. (15) As it is said, "Today, if you hear his voice, do not harden your hearts as in the rebellion." (16) For who were those who heard and yet rebelled? Was it not all those who left Egypt led by Moses? (17) And with whom was he provoked for forty years? Was it not with those who sinned, whose bodies fell in the wilderness? (18) And to whom did he swear that they would not enter his rest, but to those who were disobedient?

Jesus is greater than Moses. Moses was a servant of God but Jesus is God's Son. Jesus is the head of the temple of God of which you are if your faith and hope for rest and peace are in Christ Jesus. We hold fast to this confidence that we are the temple of God. We are that temple as faith in Jesus receives the gifts of God and makes us a dwelling of God the Holy Spirit. Our original confidence is that as Jesus is raised from the dead, He has ransomed us from death and we too shall be raised on the last day. This resurrection to eternal life he offers to all Today, right now, in this reading. You have no guarantee it will be offered tomorrow or that you will even be here tomorrow to receive it.

So Today, do not rebel like the Israelites in the desert. They were on the cusp of the Promised Land but turn away from God and did not trust God's previous promise. They feared the inhabitants of the land more than they feared God. So they traveled in the wilderness till every adult of that generation who rebelled against God had dropped dead. Will you rebel against God's promise of eternal life like them? Or will you be like Joshua and Caleb who believed the promise and were willing to go in and take the land?

Today you are offered a new heavens and a new earth, to dwell with God and Christ Jesus in righteousness where there no more evil or wickedness, a dwelling where the rain comes when it is supposed to and sun shines when it is supposed to come. The crops will come in and not be devastated by pest or nature. We will have perfect peace and rest in God and Jesus. You will be loved and you will love. Selfishness and self-centeredness will in us and others will be gone. So what will you do Today? Will you reject this offer from your Lord Jesus Christ and have the possibility of never entering his rest? Or will you rejoice and bravely go forward into the Promised Land like Joshua and Caleb not fearing the past, the present or the future? Will you look with disdain at Satan and all his minions who will try to deceive you back into fear of death? Will you say yes to sin because you know what that will get you and you're more comfortable with that than to trust in the promise the end of which we cannot see but only knowing that He who promises is faithful? Don't harden your hearts like the Israelites but trust like Joshua and believe God's promise.

Lord Jesus Christ, grant us your Holy Spirit so that as we hear your voice our hearts are not hardened but faith that burns within us to grasp hold of all that you have promised and we may walk our days here in this wilderness without fear but in your love. Amen.

Lent Day 37 Wednesday

Read Ex 10:21—11:10

Exo 10:22-23 So Moses stretched out his hand toward heaven, and there was pitch darkness in all the land of Egypt three days. (23) They did not see one another, nor did anyone rise from his place for three days, but all the people of Israel had light where they lived. Exo 11:4-5 So Moses said, "Thus says the LORD: About midnight I will go out in the midst of Egypt, (5) and every firstborn in the land of Egypt shall die, from the firstborn of Pharaoh who sits on his throne, even to the firstborn of the slave girl who is behind the hand mill, and all the firstborn of the cattle.

The plague of the firstborn calls for faith if you were going to escape it, like the plague of hail. Except for with the plague it falls upon both Egyptian and Israelite. To escape the final judgment, one must have faith in God's word, whether you were raised in the Church or not. Those who had faith put the lamb's blood on their doors that night and the firstborn lived. In like fashion, we too must have faith in Christ Jesus if we are to escape the judgment that is coming upon the world. What must we believe?

In these two plagues we see the judgment of God against His only Son, His Firstborn for the sin of the World.

On the one hand we see the darkness that covered the earth as the Father's judgment against sin is laid upon Jesus and he becomes sin for us. The Light of the World is extinguished as he becomes utter sin, darkness, and death. The Father turns His back on the Son and he cannot behold his face.

We see the wrath of the Father has he kills his firstborn. The firstborn of the Israelites were to be redeemed with blood. They belonged to the Lord. But the true firstborn, Jesus of Nazareth is called to be the substitute firstborn. The Father sacrifices Jesus on the wood of the cross so we may live.

And so while we think it was terribly cruel for God to inflict these punishments upon Egypt he laid the greater punishment upon his one and only begotten Son, Jesus, the son of Mary. This he did for you so you may escape the wrath of God where the Egyptians did not.

Lord God, Heavenly Father, we thank you for afflicting your Son Jesus instead of us so we may live to your glory. In Jesus' name we pray, Amen.

Lent Day 37 Wednesday
Read Heb 4:1–16
So then, there remains a Sabbath rest for the people of God, for whoever has entered God's rest has also rested from his works as God did from his. Let us therefore strive to enter that rest, so that no one may fall by the same sort of disobedience.
(Heb 4:9-11)

The Sabbath rest for the people of God is not any particular day of the week. It is their life. The Sabbath of the Law was a type of the rest God intended for his people. The work God intends for us to rest from is not a rest from employment, though it was typified by that in the Law. The work God intends us to rest from is all our evil works: works that are inherently evil and those "good works" which are not done in faith. These good works are those works we do by which we seek the favor of God.

But the letter to the Hebrews tells us any work done without faith in Jesus is not pleasing to God. Now that we believe Jesus is our atoning sacrifice for sin, there is no more sacrifice for us to do to be pleasing or acceptable to God.

Interestingly enough we are told to "strive" to enter that rest. The striving we do here is to remain in the faith. Remaining in the faith is a very difficult thing indeed because our flesh, the world and the devil tell us it can't be that simple, to trust in Christ's sacrifice and not our works to be pleasing to God.

In order to help us, Jesus gives us the Church where his word and sacraments strengthen and keep us in the true faith. He gives us his people there to encourage us to love and good works.

O heavenly Father, we thank you for opening up for the Sabbath rest in which we rest from our fleshly works and do the work of God, which is to believe in your Son, Jesus Christ. Continually keep us in this faith that as long as it is today we may remain faithful until we enter the heavenly city. Amen.

Maundy Thursday
Read Ex 12:1–28
Exo 12:7-8 "Then they shall take some of the blood and put it on the two doorposts and the lintel of the houses in which they eat it. (8) They shall eat the flesh that night, roasted on the fire; with unleavened bread and bitter herbs they shall eat it.

It would be a test of their faith. God had given instructions to the Israelites concerning the upcoming plague of the firstborn. They were to kill lamb, a year old, without defect. They were to put the blood on their doorposts and they were to roast the lamb whole and eat its flesh. Those who listened and believed did what the Lord said and the first born both man and beast survived that night in their homes. Those who did not believe lost loved ones that night.

Jesus is our Passover lamb. A young grown man without defect i.e. without sin, he is the one whom the Lord our God has chosen to be the sacrifice. Death claims all our lives. Not just the death of our bodies but the death of our souls. The blood of Jesus covers us in baptism. His blood upon the portals of our lips mark us a people who believe what the Lord has spoken. Because this is true, death cannot harm us. Jesus says in John, John 11:25-26 Jesus said to her, "I am the resurrection and the life. Whoever believes in me, though he die, yet shall he live, (26) and everyone who lives and believes in me shall never die. Do you believe this?"

Like the Passover lamb that is roasted whole, our Lord Jesus Christ experienced for us the eternal death, Gehennah, the Lake of Fire that is our fate for disbelieving God and disobeying him. It is written, Mat 25:41 "Then he will say to those on his left, 'Depart from me, you cursed, into the eternal fire prepared for the devil and his angels." And again, Rev 20:15 "And if anyone's name was not found written in the book of life, he was thrown into the lake of fire."

What Jesus did not suffer is for us to be suffered for our sins. Upon the cross, Jesus suffered our fate for not trusting God. And like the Passover Lamb, he gives us his body to eat in the Sacrament of Holy Communion. There his blood is place upon the door of our mouths. In partaking of this Testament, his body which suffered for us makes us whole. The angel of death looks at us and does not claim us. We have eternal life. 1Co 5:7 "… For Christ, our Passover lamb, has been sacrificed."

Heavenly Father, may we ever partake of Christ' Passover in sincerity and truth so the angel of death may Passover us and we may be made partakers of your life now and in the world to come. In Jesus' name we pray. Amen.

Maundy Thursday
Read Heb 5:1–14
Although he was a son, he learned obedience through what he suffered. And being made perfect, he became the source of eternal salvation to all who obey him, being designated by God a high priest after the order of Melchizedek.
(Heb 5:8-10)

Jesus on this day is approaching his completion. Completion is what is meant by the word perfect. Until he gives his last breath, his work is incomplete. Yet this night Jesus is completing his work. He is preparing his disciples for solid meat and weaning them from spiritual milk.

On Maundy Thursday, Jesus institutes the New Covenant: a covenant not made with the blood of bulls and goats but with his own precious blood. Now the high priest doesn't offer another's body and blood but rather our high priest offers himself. As he breaks the bread and passes the cup he gives us his own body and blood to eat and to drink. As faith receives what he is giving, it is also made partakers of the new covenant.

This new covenant is this, I will be your God and you will be my people. I will forgive you your sins and remember them no more. This perfect sacrifice of the covenant which is given us to eat and drink becomes for us the source of eternal salvation. That is if you believe what he is giving you. But if you don't believe it is judgment. The covenant demands faith. The covenant also gives the faith necessary to believe it, which is why there is judgment to those who don't believe. They have rejected the gift and the giver.

Lord Jesus we thank you for completing your good work that we may enter into eternal life. Continually give us the food of the covenant that our faith may be strengthened and persevere until the end. In your precious name we pray. Amen.

Good Friday

Read Ex 12:29–32; 13:1–16

Exo 12:29-30 At midnight the LORD struck down all the firstborn in the land of Egypt, from the firstborn of Pharaoh who sat on his throne to the firstborn of the captive who was in the dungeon, and all the firstborn of the livestock. (30) And Pharaoh rose up in the night, he and all his servants and all the Egyptians. And there was a great cry in Egypt, for there was not a house where someone was not dead.

To prepare Pharaoh to let His people go, the Lord killed all the firstborn of Egypt and Israel, both man and beast who did not believe His word. That word being, place the blood of the lamb on the lintel of your doors to preserve their lives. Those who did believe the Word of the Lord were spared.

Today we recognize and remember the death of another firstborn, the firstborn of Mary and the only begotten Son of God. Jesus, not at midnight, but at midday the sky turned dark as midnight. God the Father forsakes the Son. The Son becomes sin so we may become the righteousness of God. Jesus suffers the wrath of God there in the darkness for three hours even as Egypt was in the darkness for three days. At the ninth hour (3pm) Jesus commends His spirit to the Father and breaths out his last breath.

Now God has another promise. All who put their trust in Jesus' sacrificial death will not taste death. We have a promise that on the cross God was in Christ Jesus reconciling the world to Himself. We have the promise that all who believe and are baptized into His name will not perish but have eternal life and that this promise is for our children as well. We have the promise that Jesus' body and blood assure and deliver unto us the New Testament in which God places His law in our hearts, He becomes our God and we His people, that we would know Him and that our iniquity is forgiven and our sins are forgotten. Indeed we have the promise that if we believe in Jesus, even in His Name, we will not die but possess eternal life and even if we do die we will be raised on the last day to eternal life.

Now you have the Word of God like the Israelite and the Egyptians. If you believe it, that is you trust that this Word is true, then like the Israelites who believed the Word of the Lord and place the blood of the lamb upon their doors, then you will live eternally with God and Christ in the new heavens and new earth. If you don't believe it then you will perish likewise like the firstborn of Egypt. This is not rocket science nor is it Sisyphus' or Hercules' task. It's pretty darn simple. So, what are you going to do?

Lord Jesus Christ, on this day, by your innocent suffering death and burial, you atoned for the sin of the world. You squashed the head of Satan by obtaining for us forgiveness of our sins. You reconciled the world to the Father by the spilling of your blood. Grant us faith now to believe this and grant us your Holy Spirit that like the Israelites who believed your Word in Egypt we may live such lives which demonstrate that trust. Amen.

Good Friday

Read Heb 6:1–20

So when God desired to show more convincingly to the heirs of the promise the unchangeable character of his purpose, he guaranteed it with an oath, so that by two unchangeable things, in which it is impossible for God to lie, we who have fled for refuge might have strong encouragement to hold fast to the hope set before us. We have this as a sure and steadfast anchor of the soul, a hope that enters into the inner place behind the curtain, where Jesus has gone as a forerunner on our behalf, having become a high priest forever after the order of Melchizedek. (Heb 6:17-20)

Well that pretty much sums up the meaning of the day. God has made a promise. He swears by himself since there isn't anything higher than himself to swear by. He made a promise of salvation. He promised the promised seed would come from Abraham. He promised this seed would be a blessing to all nations. It is impossible for God to lie. In despair of our sins and our unfaithfulness, in despair of our sluggishness of faith and in our less than perfect repentance we flee refuge to Jesus for strong encouragement and to hold fast to the hope set before us.

Jesus enters the Holy of Holies this day as he gives up his last breath and the curtains of the temple split into two. Jesus enters the throne room of God in Heaven and pours out his blood on the mercy seat of God. Here he makes atonement for our sins. Here our guilt and shame is covered with his blood. Jesus is our hope that enters the inner place behind the curtain.

Now Jesus is our great high priest who intercedes for us at the right hand of God. Jesus takes the blood, his blood, the blood of the sacrifice and sprinkles it on his people to make them acceptable to God. He does this through his servants as they baptize, they absolve, they preach, they distribute the sacrament and those sprinkled share the good news. Even as the mercy seat is covered by Christ with his blood, those who will be saved must also be covered with the blood.

Jesus then is our sure and steadfast anchor of the soul. Where the soul looks to Jesus alone for his salvation it cannot be moved. It must not look at the wind and waves or clouds above. It must not look at it its own works, lack thereof, or the world and what it says. No, it must fix its eyes on Jesus, the author and perfecter of our faith. In Jesus is our only security.

Dear Jesus, as you have sacrificed yourself on this day and entered the heavenly temple with your precious blood, ever keep and perfect us in this faith of your salvific work for our soul's salvations. Amen.

Holy Saturday
Read Ex 13:17—14:9
Exo 13:17-18 When Pharaoh let the people go, God did not lead them by way of the land of the Philistines, although that was near. For God said, "Lest the people change their minds when they see war and return to Egypt." (18) But God led the people around by the way of the wilderness toward the Red Sea. And the people of Israel went up out of the land of Egypt equipped for battle.

Sometimes I am asked how come since Jesus atoned for the sins of the world on Good Friday and all who believe in him have eternal life, why does he wait so long to redeem us and bring us into Paradise. Beside the fact that he is waiting for the full number of the elect to be born and be born of the Spirit, and beside the fact he is being patient not wanting anyone to perish but that all would repent and receive eternal life, today's lesson gives us a reason for believers to keep hanging around. Even as the Israelites were not ready yet to enter the promise land for they were not prepared yet so too even though we have received eternal life, all of us whose trust is in the blood of Christ for our atonement, we are not ready to enter into God's glory just because we believe. But when we are ready then we are received. You don't want to enter into glory half-baked. St. Paul writes: 2Co 4:16-18 "So we do not lose heart. Though our outer self is wasting away, our inner self is being renewed day by day. (17) For this light momentary affliction is preparing for us an eternal weight of glory beyond all comparison, (18) as we look not to the things that are seen but to the things that are unseen. For the things that are seen are transient, but the things that are unseen are eternal." It reminds me of C.S. Lewis' "The Great Divorce" where those who have been brought to heaven have to toughen up and grow up before they can even handle walking on the grass.

Again St. Paul writes: Rom 5:3-5 "More than that, we rejoice in our sufferings, knowing that suffering produces endurance, (4) and endurance produces character, and character produces hope, (5) and hope does not put us to shame, because God's love has been poured into our hearts through the Holy Spirit who has been given to us." The Lord is still working on us. Through our walking through this wilderness like the ancient people of God, Jesus is working on producing these characteristics in you. He does this to prepare you for the day you enter into the promised-land. It is a life-long work of the Holy Spirit.

Just as the Israelites were fully armed as they entered the wilderness, to fight in the Lord their enemies who they may encounter so too we are armed and prepared for battle. (Eph 6:11-13) In this wilderness it isn't the Moabites or the Edomites we have to worry about. No our foe is Satan and all his minions who tempt us to despair of our salvation or to think we are good enough and don't need Christ. He places barriers in our way of reaching others with the good news of Jesus' all sufficient sacrifice for sins on the cross. Only with God's armor, which is the Word of God in all its forms can we stand.

Lord Jesus Christ, as we wait to enter into paradise, grant us such faith that we may persevere until the day you have fully prepared us to enter into paradise with you and the thief. Amen.

Holy Saturday
Read Heb 7:1–22

For on the one hand, a former commandment is set aside because of its weakness and uselessness (for the law made nothing perfect); but on the other hand, a better hope is introduced, through which we draw near to God. (Heb 7:18-19) This makes Jesus the guarantor of a better covenant. (Heb 7:22)

This pretty much tells us what happened Thursday and Friday. The Old Covenant with all of its laws, commandments, precepts, regulations etc. is annulled. It is abrogated. It is set aside. Yes even the Ten Commandments. St. Paul says this also in Ephesians: For he himself is our peace, who has made us both one and has broken down in his flesh the dividing wall of hostility by abolishing the law of commandments expressed in ordinances, that he might create in himself one new man in place of the two, so making peace, and might reconcile us both to God in one body through the cross, thereby killing the hostility. (Eph 2:14-16)

And in Galatians he writes: So then, the law was our guardian until Christ came, in order that we might be justified by faith. But now that faith has come, we are no longer under a guardian, for in Christ Jesus you are all sons of God, through faith. (Gal 3:24-26)

And again in Colossians: And you, who were dead in your trespasses and the uncircumcision of your flesh, God made alive together with him, having forgiven us all our trespasses, by canceling the record of debt that stood against us with its legal demands. This he set aside, nailing it to the cross. He disarmed the rulers and authorities and put them to open shame, by triumphing over them in him. Therefore let no one pass judgment on you in questions of food and drink, or with regard to a festival or a new moon or a Sabbath. These are a shadow of the things to come, but the substance belongs to Christ. (Col 2:13-17)

So be of good cheer my fellow man. We have a new covenant, a better one. Jer. 31:31ff, I will forgive you your sins and remember them no more. Therefore I will be your God and you my people. I will write my law on your hearts. Because God forgives us and forgets our sins because they are on the cross of Christ, he calls himself our God and we his people. The initiative and work is all God's. And so this is what God has left us to do in this covenant: And this is his commandment that we believe in the name of his Son Jesus Christ and love one another, just as he has commanded us. (1Jn 3:23) Such faith is a gift from God and it is he will wills and works in us such good works.

Oh heavenly Father, your mercy, kindness, and love are beyond all comprehension. Help us to believe it though that we may trust in your Son, Jesus Christ and love our neighbor as you have commanded us. Amen.

Made in the USA
Monee, IL
03 October 2024

67143448R00058